VOCABULARY CARTOONS

SAT Word Power

Learn Hundreds of SAT Words
Fast with Easy Memory Techniques

Revised & Updated Edition

New Monic Books, Inc.

Boca Raton Public Library, Boca Raton, FL

Copyright 2007 New Monic Books, Inc.

Fourth Edition

All rights reserved. No part of this work may be reproduced or transmitted in any form, or by any means, electronic or mechanical, including photocopy, recording, or any information storage and retrieval system, without written permission from the publisher. Exceptions are made for brief excerpts to be used in published reviews.

Manufactured in the United States of America.
Library of Congress Catalog Card Number: 96-96399
ISBN: 978-0-9652422-3-3
Illustrations: Joseph Toth, Lee Horton, David Horton, Luke Wilson, & John Telford
Cover Design: Bryan Burchers
Setup & Typography: Bryan Burchers & Sam Burchers III

Library of Congress Cataloging-in-Publication Data
Burchers, Sam
  Vocabutoons : Vocabulary Cartoons
  Sam Burchers, Jr., Sam Burchers, III & Bryan Burchers
      p.   cm.
  Includes index.
  ISBN 978-0-9652422-3-3
  Vocabulary Cartoons, SAT Word Power, 2nd Edition

                                                96-96399

New Monic Books
P.O. Box 511314
Punta Gorda, FL 33951
(941) 575-6669 $12.95
www.vocabularycartoons.com

Acknowledgments

The Educators

Our gratitude to the following educators in Southwest Florida who had the foresight and initiative to introduce mnemonic cartoon test programs in their schools and classrooms. It was through their efforts that vocabulary cartoons have been proven to be a dynamic new technique in building a more educated vocabulary:

North Fort Myers High School
Ed Stickles, Princ.
Larry Marsh

Alva Middle School
Jerry Demming, Asst. Princ. Cur.
Jean Riner

Cape Coral High School
Karyl Davis, Asst. Princ. Cur.
Melisa Skinner

Port Charlotte Middle School
Clyde Hoff, Princ.
Dianne Woolley

Murdock Middle School
Lou Long, Princ.
Debbie Moore
William Valella

Mariner High School
Bonnie Hill, Asst. Princ. Cur.
Judy Baxley
Jennifer Basler
Sharon Kramer
Nancy Wiseman

The Artists

Our special thanks to staff artists Joe Toth, Gene Ostmark, Bryan Burchers, Lee Horton and Dave Horton, and contributing artists Luke Wilson and John Telford. Their collective talents provided the essential quality of zany humor and outrageous bizarreness that make cartoon mnemonics memorable.

Contents

Introduction

What this book is about

Welcome to the world of humorous cartoons that introduce proven mnemonic memory techniques into the vocabulary learning experience.

A mnemonic is a device that helps you remember something by associating what you are trying to remember with something you already know. Memory experts agree that mnemonics are the surest, fastest, and easiest way to remember names places, events, words and anything else you want to remember.

If you are like most people, you want to learn words as efficiently and as rapidly as possible. With *Vocabulary Cartoons* it is possible to learn hundreds of new words over a single weekend—it's that easy!

In any public library there are numerous books on memory techniques. Without exception, experts speak of the science of mnemonics as one of the most important and basic tools of memory.

For example, U.S. Marines are taught a mnemonic based on the letters PPPFP, which means "Prior Planning Prevents Faulty Performance."

Rhymes and poems also serve as mnemonic devises. Perhaps the most common childhood mnemonic for remembering a historical date is that old limerick, "Columbus sailed the ocean blue in fourteen hundred and ninety two." Remember that one? Once you have learned it, how can you forget it?

In addition to auditory mnemonics, there are visual mnemonics, where you create in your mind's eye a mental image of whatever it is you wish to remember.

In grade school, my son, Bryan, had trouble remembering the definition of the word ALOOF.

"What does ALOOF rhyme with?" I asked him.

"ROOF," he replied.

"What's on the ROOF?"

"Our cat, Snowball," he said.

I suggested Bryan make a mental picture with both words in it. We came up with this one: "Snowball was so ALOOF, when guests came she hid on the ROOF."

Thereafter, whenever Bryan heard the word ALOOF, he would think of ROOF, then in turn visualize his cat, Snowball, hiding on the ROOF because Snowball was ALOOF.

This procedure is what the experts in memory mnemonics, such as Harry Lorayne in his book, *The Page-a-Minute Book*, recommend. Take a word you wish to learn, link it to a word, or group of words, you already know. Now visualize a mental picture of a scene in which both words play an integral part. Make the mental picture as bizarre and ridiculous as you like. Bizarre events have an impact that stimulates the memory. Commonplace events do not.

Most teachers have favorite mnemonics they pass along to their students. However, the occasional mnemonics introduced in classrooms have been used randomly and are rarely part of formal curriculum.

Now for the first time ever, we are introducing an entire book of mnemonics.

Practically all memory books ask the reader to create his or her own visual mnemonic images. With many simple words, such as our example, "aloof," it is reasonably easy to do. However, in the case of abstract words, mnemonic images can be very difficult to create.

For example, try to visualize mental picture for the word "triumvirate" and "peregrination." Anything come to mind? Probably not.

Therein lies the fallacy of visual mnemonics you are asked to conjure up yourself. The time element is devastating. You could spend hours creating appropriate visualizations for only a dozen words. The net result is most students give up on the entire mnemonic process.

Not so with *Vocabulary Cartoons,* where we provide word associations and visual images that make study easy and entertaining. You will be amazed at the magic of these specialized cartoons as your vocabulary grows and grows almost effortlessly.

Years from now, whenever you hear a word from this book, odds are the cartoon of that word will appear in your mind's eye in a flash. That is how indelible and unforgettable good mnemonics can be.

Who would benefit from this book?

Vocabulary Cartoons are designed for anyone wishing to build a stronger vocabulary. However, they are particularly recommended for students studying for Pre-Scholastic Aptitude Tests (PSAT), Scholastic Aptitude Tests (SAT), and Graduate Record Exams (GRE); older students in adult education courses, English as a Second Language (ESOL) students; those in Exceptional Student Education (ESE) programs and Attention Deficit Disorder (ADD) programs.

How to use this book

Each page has five elements:

1. The **main word**. The word you wish to learn. It is followed by the phonetic pronunciation, part of speech, and a definition.

   Example: **TRUCULENT** (TRUK yoo lunt) *adj.* inclined toward conflict; eager to fight

2. The **link word**. The link word is a simple word or phrase which rhymes or sounds like the main word.

   Example: **TRUCK YOU LENT**

3. The **caption**. The caption connects the main

word and the link word in a sentence.

Example: "The **TRUCK YOU LENT** Uncle Frank made him **TRUCULENT**."

4. The **cartoon**. The caption is illustrated in a bizarre or humorous cartoon which incorporates the main word and the link word into a visual mnemonic.

Example:

"The **TRUCK YOU LENT** Uncle Frank made him **TRUCULENT**."

5. Each cartoon is followed by two or three **sample sentences**.

Once you make the word association connection,

whenever you hear the word "TRUCULENT," the link word TRUCK YOU LENT will come to mind along with the visual image of "The TRUCK YOU LENT Uncle Frank made him TRUCULENT."

You may think of another link word that works better for you than the one provided in the book. That is okay; go ahead and use it. The main goal is to introduce you to the power of mnemonics and how well it can work for you.

Use the book like flash cards, flipping through the cartoons one by one from front to back. After a time you will find that the main word and its associating link word belong together and the visual image of the cartoon automatically appears in your mind's eye. When this happens, the definition of the main word becomes fixed in your mind.

There is an old Chinese proverb which says, "What you see once is worth what you hear a hundred times." This is another way of saying "a picture is worth a thousand words."

The words selected in this book are those most frequently found in the SAT and GRE. How well you do on the verbal skill sections of either test is exclusively determined by you vocabulary skills.

Remember that approximately 90% of university courses require reading comprehension. And to be a good reader you must have an extensive vocabulary.

School test results

The effectiveness of vocabulary mnemonics as a faster, easier learning tool has been established in six independent school tests in Southwest Florida. These tests took place in 1995 and 1996 and involved hundreds of students at different grade levels.

On average, students with *Vocabulary Cartoons*

scored 72 percent more words than the students that used the traditional rote memory studying methods. Students using *Vocabulary Cartoons* were also tested several months later to determine how effective the mnemonics were for their retention. Teachers were impressed that the students retained an average of 90 percent of the words tested. Not only did the students score well on their review tests, teachers noticed that students were more apt to identify and use those words in their studies.

Brain-friendly learning with vocabulary mnemonics

In recent years neuroscientists have uncovered astonishing facts about how the brain learns, stores, and retrieves information. The use of mnemonic applications is high on the list of the way the brain learns most naturally and efficiently. *Vocabulary Cartoon* mnemonic strategies not only accelerate learning, but they also motivate, entertain, and build self-esteem!

ABHOR
(ab HOR) *v.*
to hate very much, to detest utterly

Link: **CHORE**

"The Booker boys ABHORRED doing CHORES."

❑ To **ABHOR** insects is to find them **ABHORRENT**.

❑ It is generally believed that most women have an **ABHORRENCE** of mice.

❑ It is a fact that most people **ABHOR** the thought of public speaking.

ABOMINATE
(uh BOM uh nate) *v.*
extreme hatred, loathing

Link: **A BOMB HATE**

"I ABOMINATE BOMBS."

- ❑ Laura **ABOMINATES** vegetables, she would try anything so she wouldn't have to eat them.

- ❑ Sylvia **ABOMINATED** her relatives when they came to visit and tracked mud on her new white carpet.

- ❑ (An **ABOMINATION** is something despised.) The movie was a total **ABOMINATION**, we walked out of the theatre after just thirty minutes.

ABRIDGE
(uh BRIJ) *v.*
to shorten; to condense;
to diminish; to curtail

Link: **BRIDGE**

*"An **ABRIDGED BRIDGE**."*

- ❏ If you don't want to read an entire newspaper to learn the latest daily news, there are clipping services that will **ABRIDGE** news stories to your specifications.

- ❏ An **ABRIDGED** dictionary is one that has been shortened.

- ❏ We saw an **ABRIDGEMENT** of the movie *Gone With the Wind* on TV last night; it only lasted two hours whereas the original lasted four.

ABSTRUSE
(ab STROOS) *adj.*
hard to understand

Link: **MOOSE**

"His friends consider Mike, the
MOOSE*, to be very* ***ABSTRUSE.****"*

- ❏ Chemistry is an **ABSTRUSE** subject of study for many students.

- ❏ The scientists had many **ABSTRUSE** theories about atomic interactions.

- ❏ Elizabeth's directions to the party were very **ABSTRUSE**.

ABUT
(uh BUT) *v.*
to border upon; to adjoin

Link: **BUTT**

"ABUTTING BUTTS"

- ❏ In Hong Kong the skyscrapers so closely **ABUT** each other, in some cases they touch sides.

- ❏ Texas **ABUTS** Mexico on its southern border.

- ❏ The **ABUTTING** rocks formed a perfect wall for riflemen to defend the castle.

ABYSS
(uh BISS) *n.*
bottomless pit; a yawning gulf;
a profound depth or void

Link: **MISS**

*"The diver **MISSED** the ledge and
sank deep into the **ABYSS**."*

- ❏ The lost spaceship wandered endlessly in the vast **ABYSS** of the galaxy.

- ❏ After the rescuers dug without success for three days through the snow of the avalanche in search of the missing skier, they were disheartened and faced an emotional **ABYSS** of despair.

- ❏ Staring down the **ABYSS** of the mine shaft we were uncertain of how deep it really was.

ACCOLADE
(AK uh layd) *n.*
an award, an honor; approval, praise

Link: **LEMONADE**

*"Jane and Jack received ACCOLADES
for their LEMONADE."*

- ❏ Laura received **ACCOLADES** from her parents when she brought home her report card with straight As.

- ❏ The **ACCOLADES** she received for making the varsity swim team quickly went to her head.

- ❏ After running in his first marathon, Mike said he didn't do it for the **ACCOLADES**, he just wanted to get back in shape.

ADJUNCT
(AJ unkt) *n.*
something connected or added to another
in a subordinate position; an assistant

Link: **ADD JUNK**

*"The tank driver ADDED JUNK as
an ADJUNCT to his tank."*

- ☐ Hang gliding is only an **ADJUNCT** to Roseanna's real love, which is skydiving.

- ☐ The library was an **ADJUNCT** to the Blakemores' original home.

- ☐ The general's adjutant was not an **ADJUNCT**, but a permanent part of his staff command.

AFFIDAVIT
(af uh DAY vit) *n.*
a sworn written statement

Link: **AFTER DAVID**

*"**AFTER DAVID** slew Goliath, he made out an **AFFIDAVIT** not to further hurt any big guys."*

❏ The defense lawyer had a sworn **AFFIDAVIT** from witnesses claiming his client was innocent of the crime charged against him.

❏ Roseanne had an **AFFIDAVIT** from her neighbor giving her permission to cut down the tree on their mutual property line.

❏ The chairman accepted an **AFFIDAVIT** from the claimant, who was too ill to appear before the county commission.

AFFINITY
(uh FIN uh tee) *n.*
a natural attraction; kinship; similarity

Link: **FIN TEA**

*"The Chinese have an **AFFINITY** for shark fin soup and shark **FIN TEA**."*

- ❑ Max had an **AFFINITY** for sports and excelled at football, basketball, and tennis.

- ❑ Monkeys have an **AFFINITY** for climbing, birds for flying, and fish for swimming.

- ❑ A natural **AFFINITY** exists between monkeys and apes.

VOCABULARY CARTOONS Review #1

Match the word with its definition.

___ 1. **abhor**	a. hard to understand
___ 2. **abominate**	b. a sworn written statement
___ 3. **abridge**	c. bottomless pit
___ 4. **abstruse**	d. to hate very much
___ 5. **abut**	e. a natural attraction
___ 6. **abyss**	f. to border upon
___ 7. **accolade**	g. to shorten
___ 8. **adjunct**	h. something added
___ 9. **affidavit**	i. extreme hatred
___ 10. **affinity**	j. an honor; praise

Fill in the blanks with the most appropriate word. The word form may need changing.

1. Texas _____ Mexico on its southern border.

2. An _____ dictionary is one that has been shortened.

3. Laura _____ vegetables, she would try anything so she wouldn't have to eat them.

4. The defense lawyer had a sworn _____ from witnesses claiming his client was innocent of the crime charged against him.

5. Staring down the _____ of the mine shaft we were uncertain of how deep it really was.

6. It is a fact that most people _____ the thought of public speaking.

7. A natural _____ exists between monkeys and apes.

8. After running in his first marathon, Mike said he didn't do it for the _____ he just wanted to get back in shape.

9. The library was an _____ to the Blakemores' original home.

10. Chemistry is an _____ subject of study for many students.

25

AFTERMATH
(AF tur math) *n.*
events following some occurrence;
a consequence of

Link: **AFTER MATH**

*"**AFTER** doing the **MATH** for calculating
the atomic bomb, Einstein would live to
see the resulting **AFTERMATH**.*

❑ Poverty and economic depression are usually the
AFTERMATH of wars.

❑ An **AFTERMATH** of the bombing of Hiroshima
was thousands of cancer cases caused by
radiation.

❑ The **AFTERMATH** of Christina skipping classes
too often to practice ballet was flunking Chemistry
101.

AGGRANDIZE
(uh GRAN dize) *v.*
to increase in size; enlarge, to cause
to appear greater in power, influence

Link: **GRAND EYES**

*"Ladies acquire **GRAND EYES** with mascara and false eyelashes to **AGGRANDIZE** their eyes."*

❑ To **AGGRANDIZE** his achievements Richard would make up unbelievable stories of personal accomplishments.

❑ The greatest **AGGRANDIZEMENT** of the entire evening was when the Russian claimed that Russia had won World War II without any help from the United States or the other allies.

❑ Mario **AGGRANDIZED** his wealth by borrowing so much money and buying extravagant homes, cars, and boats that it eventually bankrupted him.

AJAR
(uh JARR) *n.*
partially open

Link: **JAR**

*"Hey, the **JAR'S AJAR**; we're outta here."*

- When the police carefully examined the crime scene, they found a window had been left **AJAR**.

- Even though Mr. Kreamer had rejected the offer to sell his hardware store, he left the offer **AJAR** by saying he would reconsider after the Christmas season.

- By leaving the front door of the house **AJAR**, hundreds of mosquitoes kept me awake all night long.

ALIENATE
(AY lee uh nate) *v.*
to make hostile; to cause to feel
unwelcome or estranged

Link: **ALIEN ATE**

*"The chief ALIEN ATE all the ice cream
and ALIENATED his crew."*

❏ The boss **ALIENATED** his secretary by shouting
at her when she made a mistake.

❏ All during school, Bob Smith felt **ALIENATED** by
the other students because he wore his hair down
to his knees.

❏ Barb was **ALIENATED** from her group when they
learned that she was the town gossip.

ALLEVIATE
(uh LEE vee ayt) *v.*
to make less severe;
to relieve, to lessen

Link: **LEAVES ATE**

*"The natives believed if they **ATE** the **LEAVES** of some trees it would **ALLEVIATE** many illnesses."*

- ❑ When Peter arrived with sacks of ice for the party, it **ALLEVIATED** the need to wait for the icemaker to produce more.

- ❑ When the team stopped for lunch, our coach **ALLEVIATED** the need for the waitress to bring separate checks when she offered to pay for all of us as a gesture of congratulations for our victory.

- ❑ Aspirin **ALLEVIATES** painful headaches most of the time.

ALLURE
(uh LUHR) *v./n.*
to entice with something desirable;
tempt; power of attraction

Link: **LURE**

"Not all fish **LURES ALLURE** all fish."

❑ The actress **ALLURED** the crowd with her over-whelming beauty.

❑ The sailors were **ALLURED** into believing that the calm, balmy seas would never become a ferocious storm.

❑ Psychologists find it puzzling, but all agree that movie stars have some indescribable **ALLURING** quality that movie audiences find irresistible.

ALOOF

(uh LOOF) *adj.*
distant, reserved in
manner; uninvolved

Link: **ROOF**

*"The cat is so **ALOOF**, when guests
come she hides on the **ROOF**."*

❑ Most everyone thought Theodore **ALOOF** when
actually he was only very shy.

❑ Nothing ruins a fine dinner at a good restaurant
like an **ALOOF** waiter who makes the entire
experience uncomfortable.

❑ At the wedding reception, the bride's relatives
were very **ALOOF**, hardly speaking to the groom's
guests and family.

ALSO-RAN
(AWL so ran) *n.*
one who is defeated in a race,
election, or other competition; loser

Link: **AWESOME FAN**

*"The tortoise was an **ALSO-RAN** until he
strapped on an **AWESOME FAN**."*

❑ Even though George Bush received millions of
votes in the presidential election, he was an
ALSO-RAN to Bill Clinton.

❑ With twenty thousand runners in the New York
Marathon, even if you come in second place, you
would still be an **ALSO-RAN**.

❑ Tired of always being an **ALSO-RAN**, Mike
trained hard and finally won the annual club
tennis tournament.

ALTERCATION
(awl tur KAY shun) *n.*
a heated quarrel

Link: **ALTAR**

*"An **ALTERCATION** at the wedding **ALTAR**"*

- ❑ The Mafia had a slight **ALTERCATION** with the police, and ten gang members were arrested and booked in downtown Manhattan.

- ❑ The Sioux Indians were not looking for an **ALTERCATION**, but when General Custer's men attacked their village, the Sioux wiped out Custer and his troops in self-defense.

- ❑ When the pitcher hit the batter with a fastball an **ALTERCATION** soon broke out between both teams.

ALTERNATIVE
(all TUR nah tiv) *n.*
the choice between two mutually exclusive
possibilities, a situation presenting such a choice

Link: **TURN NATIVE**

*"It's an **ALTERNATIVE** life style;
he **TURNED NATIVE**."*

❏ "I've had six by-pass operations," said Harry. "It's
no fun, but better than the **ALTERNATIVE**."

❏ The **ALTERNATIVE** to playing in the band was to
go out for the football team.

❏ The hikers decided there was no **ALTERNATIVE**;
they had to find shelter before the rains came.

Match the word with its definition.

___ 1. **aftermath**   a. to cause to feel unwelcome
___ 2. **aggrandize**   b. a consequence of
___ 3. **ajar**   c. partially open
___ 4. **alienate**   d. choice between two possibilities
___ 5. **alleviate**   e. a heated quarrel
___ 6. **allure**   f. to make less severe
___ 7. **aloof**   g. one who is defeated
___ 8. **also-ran**   h. to exaggerate
___ 9. **altercation**   i. to entice
___ 10. **alternative**   j. distant, reserved in manner

Fill in the blanks with the most appropriate word. The word form may need changing.

1. Barb was _____ from her group when they learned that she was the town gossip.

2. Tired of always being an _____, Mike trained hard and finally won the annual club tennis tournament.

3. To _____ his achievements Richard would make up unbelievable stores of personal accomplishments.

4. When the pitcher hit the batter with a fastball an _____ soon broke out between both teams.

5. The actress _____ the crowd with her overwhelming beauty.

6. An _____ of the bombing of Hiroshima was thousands of cancer cases caused by radiation.

7. The _____ to playing in the band was to go out for the football team.

8. By leaving the front door of the house _____, hundreds of mosquitoes kept me awake all night long.

9. At the wedding reception, the bride's relatives were very _____, hardly speaking to the groom's guests and family.

10. Aspirin _____ painful headaches most of the time.

AMBIANCE
(AM bee uns) *n.*
mood, feeling; general atmosphere

Link: **AMBULANCE**

"George did not enjoy the
***AMBIANCE** in the **AMBULANCE**."*

❏ The **AMBIANCE** of the locker room after the team lost the championship was depressing.

❏ For their daughter's birthday party, the Jeffersons created an **AMBIANCE** of gaiety, decorating the garden with bright balloons and ribbons.

❏ The **AMBIANCE** in the Italian restaurant was delightful, there was soft music, candlelight, and singing waiters.

AMENABLE

(ah MEE nuh bul) *adj.*
agreeable, responsible to authority, pleasant,
willing to give in to the wishes of another

Link: **MEAN BULL**

"The matador tried to be
AMENABLE to the MEAN BULL."

- ❑ Jack was such a classy guy, always **AMENABLE** to any reasonable solution to a problem.

- ❑ The **AMENABLE** young man helped the old lady carry her groceries to her car.

- ❑ Sarah was **AMENABLE** to calling back tomorrow when the office would be open.

AMPLIFY
(AM pluh fie) *v.*
to make larger, louder, or more powerful

Link: **ANTS AND FLIES**

*"Dr. Frankie AMPLIFIED the ANTS
AND FLIES to a monstrous proportion."*

❏ The music was **AMPLIFIED** to the point where the guests couldn't hear themselves speak.

❏ General Rommel was unable to **AMPLIFY** the role of his tank corps in the battle of El Alamein because he didn't have fuel to run them.

❏ Some actors attempt to **AMPLIFY** their roles by upstaging their fellow actors.

ANTECEDENT

(an tuh SEED unt) *n.*
going before; preceding; an occurrence
or event preceding another

Link: **HAND SEED**

"The HAND that plants the SEED is the
ANTECEDENT to the hand that picks the flower."

- ❏ The steam engine was the **ANTECEDENT** to the gasoline engine.

- ❏ Your ancestors were your **ANTECEDENTS**.

- ❏ The atomic bomb was the **ANTECEDENT** to the hydrogen bomb.

ANTERIOR

(an TEER ee ur) *adj.*
situated in front

Link: **ANTLERS**

*"The ANTERIOR position of a deer's
ANTLERS comes in very handy."*

- ❑ There is the **ANTERIOR** up front, the interior inside, the exterior outside, and the posterior bringing up the rear.

- ❑ The **ANTERIOR** of a stage is not as interesting as what takes place behind the scenes.

- ❑ The **ANTERIOR** of a ship is called the bow.

APPALLING

(uh PAWL ing) *adj.*
filling with dismay; causing
horror or consternation; shock

Link: **FALLING**

*"Sue had an **APPALLING** dream
that she was **FALLING**."*

❏ It was absolutely **APPALLING** the way Jews were
treated in Nazi Germany during World War II.

❏ The travelers received an **APPALLING** reception
at the village hotel; they were given the smallest
rooms for the highest prices.

❏ Karen had an **APPALLED** look on her face after
seeing the destruction the hurricane had caused
to her house.

APTITUDE
(AP tuh tude) *n.*
capacity for learning; natural ability

Link: ALTITUDE

"Birds have an APTITUDE for ALTITUDE."

- ❑ Chris has had a champion's **APTITUDE** for tennis since she was four years old.

- ❑ Jess is all thumbs and has no **APTITUDE** for fixing things around the house.

- ❑ Laura has an **APTITUDE** for numbers, ever since she was young she always received high marks in math class.

ARCHAIC

(ahr KAY ik) *adj.*
belonging to an earlier
time, ancient; outdated

Link: **CAKE**

*"An **ARCHAIC CAKE**"*

❑ Her parents had an absolutely **ARCHAIC** idea of dating. She not only had to be in by nine o'clock, but her aunt chaperoned her on all her dates.

❑ **ARCHAIC** civilizations, those that aren't around anymore, are the chief subject of archaeological studies.

❑ Underdeveloped countries that depend on agriculture for their economy will never raise their standard of living as long as they use **ARCHAIC** farm tools.

ARDUOUS
(AHR joo us) *adj.*
hard, difficult, tiresome

Link: **HARD ON US**

*"The **ARDUOUS** snow-covered
trail is **HARD ON US**."*

❑ The assignment given the recruits was an
ARDUOUS twenty mile hike with full packs in the
hot sun.

❑ Swimming three miles was the most **ARDUOUS**
exercise Jeannie ever had.

❑ The long, **ARDUOUS** boat trip was made even
worse by stormy seas and much seasickness.

ARTISAN

(AHR tih sun) *n.*
a worker skilled in a craft

Link: **ART IN SAND**

"Little Jimmy was a SAND CASTLE ARTISAN."

- ❑ The **ARTISANS** of Pueblo, Mexico are known for their beautiful pottery.

- ❑ The **ARTISANS** arrived early in the morning to repaint and landscape the house.

- ❑ The Italian painter and sculptor Michelangelo was both an artist and an **ARTISAN**.

VOCABULARY CARTOONS Review #3

Match the word with its definition.

___ 1. **ambiance**
___ 2. **amenable**
___ 3. **amplify**
___ 4. **antecedent**
___ 5. **anterior**
___ 6. **appalling**
___ 7. **aptitude**
___ 8. **archaic**
___ 9. **arduous**
___ 10. **artisan**

a. ancient; outdated
b. filling with dismay
c. to make larger
d. general atmosphere
e. agreeable
f. going before
g. hard, difficult
h. natural ability
i. a worker skilled in a craft
j. situated in front

Fill in the blanks with the most appropriate word. The word form may need changing.

1. The steam engine was the _____ to the gasoline engine.

2. The _____ in the Italian restaurant was delightful, there was soft music, candlelight, and singing waiters.

3. Laura has an _____ for numbers, every since she was young she always received high marks in math class.

4. The _____ young man helped the old lady carry her groceries to her car.

5. The _____ of Pueblo, Mexico are known for their beautiful pottery.

6. The assignment given the recruits was an _____ twenty mile hike with full packs in the hot sun.

7. The _____ of a ship is called the bow.

8. The music was _____ to the point where the guests couldn't hear themselves speak.

9. Underdeveloped countries that depend on agriculture for their economy will never raise their standard of living as long as they use _____ farm tools.

10. Karen had an _____ look on her face after seeing the destruction the hurricane had caused to her house.

47

ASKEW
(uh SKYOO) *adj.*
to one side; crooked; awry;
a sidelong look of contempt

Link: **CUE**

"Curly's pool CUE had become ASKEW."

- ❑ After the flood receded, the bridge was found to be **ASKEW** of the road which connected to it.

- ❑ The tire wouldn't fit on the car because in the accident the axle had been bent **ASKEW**.

- ❑ The speaker looked **ASKEW** at the heckler at every interruption.

ASPIRE
(uh SPIRE) *v.*
to seek, attain, or achieve a goal

Link: **RETIRE**

*"Jim **ASPIRED** to **RETIRE** early and become a man of leisure."*

❑ Tim **ASPIRED** to be the valedictorian of his class at graduation and studied hard to reach that goal.

❑ The counselor told Jim's parents that his problem in school was he didn't **ASPIRE** for anything. He had no goals or career direction.

❑ As a young child, General Custer had **ASPIRED** to become a musician, but later decided to become a general instead.

ASSUAGE
(uh SWAYJ) *v.*
to soothe; to make less severe;
to satisfy, ease, lessen

Link: **MASSAGE**

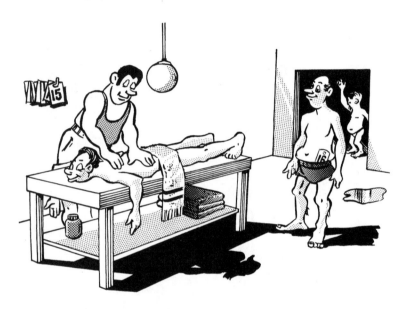

*"A good **MASSAGE** is known to **ASSUAGE** sore muscles and relieve uptight feelings."*

- ❑ When Jane double faulted on match point, her coach came to her side and tried to **ASSUAGE** her disappointment by telling her she played a great tournament, and that no one is perfect.

- ❑ Dr. Moore was able to **ASSUAGE** the fear of his patient by predicting successful treatment.

- ❑ Many athletes drink sport drinks to **ASSUAGE** their thirst.

ASTUTE
(uh STEWT) *adj.*
quick in discernment; shrewd, clever, keen

Link: **SUIT**

*"Larry thought a new **SUIT** would make him appear more **ASTUTE** for his job interview."*

❑ Louisa has a natural **ASTUTENESS** in dealing with angry people and winning them over to her view, thereby settling matters amicably.

❑ Like many gamblers, John thought he was very **ASTUTE** when it came to betting on horses. Only his wife kept telling him if he was so **ASTUTE**, he would realize he lost more often than he won.

❑ Mary was known to be very **ASTUTE**. She was always the first to finish her assignments.

ASUNDER

(uh SUN dur) *adj.*
in separate parts; apart from
each other in position

Link: **THUNDER**

*"The lightning and **THUNDER** tore
the young lovers **ASUNDER**."*

❑ When the earthquake stopped, and we came up
from our shelter, we found the city had been torn
ASUNDER and not one single building was left
standing.

❑ Our team lost its unity and became a group of
individuals who played entirely for themselves,
ASUNDER from each other.

❑ The curtains had been drawn **ASUNDER**.

ATROPHY
(AT ruh fee) *v.*
to wither away

Link: **TROPHY**

*"Once a **TROPHY** champion, Jim's muscles
ATROPHIED due to a chronic illness."*

- ❏ The author's interest in writing **ATROPHIED** after he won the Pulitzer Prize for literature.

- ❏ The **ATROPHIC** condition of the mummy was apparent as soon as the tomb was opened.

- ❏ The **ATROPHIED** bodies of the starving children were an appalling sight.

ATYPICAL
(ay TIP uh kull) *adj.*
not typical, abnormal

Link: **TYPICAL**

"Uncle Jeff's old bicycle is not
***TYPICAL** of bikes today, it is **ATYPICAL**."*

- A banana without a curve in its length is **ATYPICAL** of the species.

- His parents agreed it was most **ATYPICAL** of John to stay home and study Saturday night when he could have gone to the movies with his friends.

- It was an **ATYPICAL** decision for our boss to give us the day off with pay.

AUSTERE
(aw STEER) *adj.*
stern, as in manner; without excess,
unadorned, severely simple and plain

Link: **STEER**

*"An **AUSTERE STEER**
is no fun at a party."*

❏ Mike's **AUSTERE** dorm room only had one chair
and a mattress.

❏ The **AUSTERITY** of life in the village was under-
standable. Many were jobless and evidence of
poverty was everywhere.

❏ Her home was **AUSTERELY** decorated, with very
plain furniture without frills and only items that
were necessary.

BADGER
(BAJ er) *v.*
to tease, annoy, harass persistently

Link: **BADGER**

"A BADGERING BADGER"

❑ "Don't **BADGER** me," Louis said to his daughter. "I promised I'd take you to the mall, so please be patient until I finish my work."

❑ The school bully **BADGERED** Rog endlessly, until one day Rog became so provoked that he socked him in the mouth.

❑ I hate to be **BADGERED** by phone solicitors.

BALLISTICS
(buh LISS ticks) *n.*
the study of the dynamics or flight
characteristics of projectiles

Link: **LIPSTICK**

"BALLISTIC LIPSTICK"

- ❑ **BALLISTICS** is a noun, while **BALLISTIC** is an adjective which means "of projectiles."

- ❑ Most naval warships carry **BALLISTIC** missiles.

- ❑ Detective Culleton specializes in **BALLISTICS** and is always called to a crime scene whenever a firearm is involved.

VOCABULARY CARTOONS Review #4

Match the word with its definition.

___ 1. **askew**		a. to tease, annoy, harass
___ 2. **aspire**		b. severely simple and plain
___ 3. **assuage**		c. in separate parts
___ 4. **astute**		d. the study of the flight of projectiles
___ 5. **asunder**		e. to soothe; to make less severe
___ 6. **atrophy**		f. crooked; awry
___ 7. **atypical**		g. to wither away
___ 8. **austere**		h. shrewd, clever, keen
___ 9. **badger**		i. not typical, abnormal
___ 10. **ballistics**		j. to seek, attain, or achieve a goal

Fill in the blanks with the most appropriate word.
The word form may need changing.

1. Tim _____ to be the valedictorian of his class at graduation and studied hard to reach that goal.

2. Mike's _____ dorm room only had one chair and a mattress.

3. The curtains had been drawn _____.

4. A banana without a curve in its length is _____ of the species.

5. Many athletes drink sport drinks to _____ their thirst.

6. I hate to be _____ by phone solicitors.

7. The tire wouldn't fit on the car because in the accident the axle had been bent _____.

8. Mary was known to be very _____. She was always the first to finish her assignments.

9. Detective Culleton specializes in _____ and is always called to a crime scene whenever a firearm is involved.

10. The _____ bodies of the starving children were an appalling sight.

BALM
(balm) *adj./n.*
something that heals or comforts;
soothing; an oil or ointment

Link: **PALM**

*"There's nothing like a **BALMY** breeze
whispering through **PALM** trees."*

❑ The nurse gave me a white **BALM** to put on my
insect bites to soothe the pain.

❑ It was a **BALMY** day, perfect for a game of golf
or a trip to the beach.

❑ After sweating through his final exams, the sound
of the bell at the end of class was a **BALM** to
Pete's nerves.

BEGET
(bee GET) *v.*
to give birth to; to create

Link: **FORGET**

*"The old lady who lived in the shoe **BEGAT** so many children she would **FORGET** who was who."*

- ❑ Prior to the development of large farm machinery, farmers used to **BEGET** large families to help them run their farms.

- ❑ Chronic lying becomes a habit which starts out with one small lie, which **BEGETS** a second lie, which **BEGETS** a third lie, and so on.

- ❑ The Wright brothers didn't invent the airplane, but they were the **BEGETTERS** of the first sustained flight in the United States.

BELEAGUER

(be LEE gur) *v.*
to besiege; beset, surround, harass

Link: **BIG LEAGUER**

*"The little leaguers BELEAGUERED
the BIG LEAGUERS."*

- ❏ In World War II, the Russian city of Stalingrad was **BELEAGUERED** by the German Army for five months before it fell to the Germans.

- ❏ During his last year in office, Richard Nixon was a **BELEAGUERED** president, struggling to fight off the Watergate scandal.

- ❏ In the midst of important negotiations, the union official asked his staff not to **BELEAGUER** him with insignificant details.

BEREAVE
(buh REEV) *v./adj.*
suffering the death of
a loved one; left alone

Link: **LEAVE**

*"He was **BEREAVED** when his fish had to **LEAVE**."*

- ❑ When their pony died, the **BEREAVED** children were told by their mother that everyone dies, and it was all right to cry and feel sad for a time.

- ❑ At his funeral procession, Jacqueline Kennedy's **BEREAVEMENT** over the death of her husband, President John F. Kennedy, was recorded on television for the entire nation to see.

- ❑ The **BEREAVED** widow wore a black dress to her husband's funeral.

BESET
(bee SET) *v.*
to harass; to surround

Link: **BEES SAT**

*"The angry **BEES SAT** on his face
and **BESET** the beekeeper."*

- ❏ We were to have gone to the beach for a sunny vacation, but were **BESET** with a week of rain and cold weather.

- ❏ We thought we had the design ironed out, but when three of our aircraft crashed, we knew we were **BESET** with design problems we had yet to understand.

- ❏ The losing team was **BESET** with disappointment.

BIZARRE
(bih ZAR) *adj.*
extremely unconventional
or far-fetched

Link: **BAZAAR**

*"You see some **BIZARRE**
things for sale at a **BAZAAR**."*

❑ It was a **BIZARRE** set of events that led to the
violinist being in the small Swiss village, for it was
here he met a young flutist who was to become
his wife.

❑ As the medication began to take effect,
Randolph's eyes took on a faraway look, and he
muttered some **BIZARRE** nonsense about
wanting to ride the pony one more time.

❑ "Wasn't he **BIZARRE**?" Lorna said of the strange
man who appeared from nowhere and offered her
an apple.

BLATHER
(BLA thur) *v.*
to talk nonsensically

Link: **LATHER**

*"Karen and Allison **BLATHERED** until
their mouths **LATHERED**."*

❑ Everything the media reported about the supposed plane disaster never happened. It was a bunch of **BLATHER** by uninformed journalists.

❑ Children have great imaginations, and often **BLATHER** about ghosts that supposedly enter their rooms and either scare them or play with them.

❑ All Mary likes to do is **BLATHER** with her friends on the phone.

BLEAK

(bleek) *adj.*
depressing, discouraging,
harsh, cold, barren, raw

Link: **LEAK**

*"Sometimes a simple LEAK can
lead to BLEAK consequences."*

- ❏ The game looked **BLEAK** with our team being down 42 to 7 in the fourth quarter.

- ❏ The vet said we should keep our hopes up, but the chance of our dog, Spot, surviving the car accident appeared **BLEAK**.

- ❏ The **BLEAKNESS** of the Aleutian Islands, where the winds howl constantly, makes one shiver just to see a picture of it.

BLUDGEON
(BLUD jun) *v./n.*
to hit or attack with heavy impact;
a short, heavy thick club that has
one end larger than the other

Link: **DUNGEON**

"Why do you suppose they have all these
***BLUDGEONS** in this **DUNGEON**?"*

- There was nothing temperate about the lawyer's summary to the jury; he **BLUDGEONED** them with all the gruesome details of the murder.

- The detective suspected the murder weapon was some type of **BLUDGEON**.

- The police arrested the lumberjack on suspicion of **BLUDGEONING** a co-worker with an axe handle.

BUCOLIC
(byoo KAHL ik) *adj.*
rural or rustic in
nature, country-like

Link: **BULLS FROLIC**

"BULLS FROLIC when a farm is BUCOLIC."

- ❑ The judges gave first prize to the painting of a **BUCOLIC** landscape in greens and blues.

- ❑ There is nothing **BUCOLIC** about big city life, honking horns and bustling streets are neither peaceful or rustic.

- ❑ Mr. Pride's farm with its peaceful green pastures and a babbling brook, was the perfect **BUCOLIC** setting for a picnic.

VOCABULARY CARTOONS Review #5

Match the word with its definition.

___ 1. **balm**
___ 2. **beget**
___ 3. **beleaguer**
___ 4. **bereave**
___ 5. **beset**
___ 6. **bizarre**
___ 7. **blather**
___ 8. **bleak**
___ 9. **bludgeon**
___ 10. **bucolic**

a. to surround
b. to harass
c. a short, heavy thick club
d. soothing
e. to talk nonsensically
f. depressing, discouraging, harsh
g. rural or rustic in nature
h. extremely unconventional
i. suffering the death of a loved one
j. to give birth to

Fill in the blanks with the most appropriate word. The word form may need changing.

1. All Mary likes to do is _____ with her friends on the phone.

2. "Wasn't he _____?" Lorna said of the strange man who appeared from nowhere and offered her an apple.

3. The _____ widow wore a black dress to her husband's funeral.

4. It was a _____ day, perfect for a game of golf or a trip to the beach.

5. The detective suspected the murder weapon was some type of _____.

6. Mr. Pride's farm with its peaceful green pastures and a babbling brook, was the perfect _____ setting for a picnic.

7. The game looked _____ with our team being down 42 to 7 in the fourth quarter.

8. During his last year in office, Richard Nixon was a _____ president, struggling to fight off the Watergate scandal.

9. Prior to the development of large farm machinery, farmers used to _____ large families to help them run their farms.

10. The losing team was _____ with disappointment.

BULWARK
(BULL wurk) *n.*
a defensive wall; something serving
as a principal defense

Link: **BULL WORK**

"BULLS WORK building a BULWARK."

- ❑ Quebec City is the only city in North America with a **BULWARK** built entirely around it.

- ❑ The budget for national defense is an economic burden for all taxpayers, but we must never forget our armed services are the **BULWARK** of defense for the nation.

- ❑ Our mother was a **BULWARK** against bad times; no matter how bad things became she always wore a smile and had a cheerful word.

CACHE
(kash) *n.*
a hiding place, or the objects
hidden in a hiding place

Link: **CASH**

*"Escaped prisoner #5447 recovered
the CASH from his CACHE."*

❏ Treasure hunters have searched for Blackbeard's
treasure in Bahamian caves, but no one has yet
found his **CACHE**.

❏ Mom found a **CACHE** of candy behind Laura's
bed. No wonder she doesn't eat much dinner.

❏ The police uncovered a **CACHE** of weapons and
money at the gang's hideout.

CACOPHONY
(kuh KAH fuh nee) *n.*
harsh sounds

Link: **COUGH**

*"A **CACOPHONY** of **COUGHING**"*

- ❑ A **CACOPHONY** isn't just noise, it is disturbing noise such as when people shout all at once.

- ❑ Grandpa thinks all rock music is a **CACOPHONY** to be avoided whenever possible.

- ❑ An unpleasant **CACOPHONY** of sound was produced as the orchestra tuned their instruments. But once they began to play together the sounds became euphonious.

CAJOLE

(kuh JOHL) *v.*
to wheedle, coax, or persuade someone
to do something they didn't want to

Link: **PAROLE**

*"Jimmy the Geek tried to CAJOLE the
warden into giving him PAROLE."*

- ❑ Allison **CAJOLED** me into entering the marathon just so she could get a free T-shirt.

- ❑ Some of the younger Republicans were **CAJOLED** into voting for the Democratic candidate because he promised to lower the voting age.

- ❑ Jeannie always sweet-talked and **CAJOLED** her parents into letting her have her way.

CALLOUS

(KAL us) *adj.*
unfeeling, insensitive

Link: **CALLUS**

*"Jack was so CALLOUS, he called
attention to Mike's CALLUSES."*

❑ A **CALLOUS** remark about someone does not
take into consideration his or her feelings.

❑ One is sometimes **CALLOUS** to people begging
on street corners.

❑ The **CALLOUS** movie star would not sign
autographs or even acknowledge her fans.

CALLOW
(KAL oh) *adj.*
immature and inexperienced

Link: **SHALLOW**

*"Our dad was so **CALLOW** he made his first dive in our **SHALLOW** kiddie pool."*

☐ The **CALLOW** appearance of the troops he now inspected reminded General Troister that wars kill the youth of the nation, not the old politicians who start them.

☐ The **CALLOW** boater did not have a life preserver, paddle, or radio onboard his sailboat.

☐ **CALLOW** she was, but you never saw a more enthusiastic, hard working young lady at the glove factory.

CANDOR
(CAN dur) *n.*
truthfulness, sincere honesty

Link: **CONDOR**

"A CONDOR with CANDOR"

- ❏ Speaking with **CANDOR**, the governor called for police reforms throughout the state.

- ❏ Without regard to feelings, our teacher said she would criticize our term papers with absolute **CANDOR**.

- ❏ The coach told his team that **CANDOR** means to speak honestly, and to speak **CANDIDLY**, the team stunk. (**CANDID** means showing **CANDOR**.)

CAPACIOUS
(kuh PAY shus) *adj.*
roomy, able to hold much

Link: **CAP SPACIOUS**

"A SPACIOUS CAP is CAPACIOUS."

❑ The old castle has a **CAPACIOUS** dining room large enough to seat a small army.

❑ David's memory for jokes is **CAPACIOUS**; he remembers them all.

❑ Our bed at the hotel was really **CAPACIOUS**; all three sisters slept there.

CASTIGATE
(KAS tuh gate) *v.*
to criticize harshly, usually with the
intention of correcting wrongdoing

Link: **PASSED THE GATE**

*"The gate attendant CASTIGATED
Herman for PASSING THE GATE."*

- The coach was **CASTIGATED** by the university's administration for not recruiting football players in compliance with NCAA regulations.

- Jimmy's mother **CASTIGATED** him for tracking mud on their new living room carpet.

- When **CASTIGATED** for behavior unbecoming of a naval officer, Chief Petty Officer Peterson was denied shore-leave.

CATAPULT
(KAT uh pult) *v./n.*
to launch; a device for
hurling objects, a slingshot

Link: **CAT**

"Testing the first CAT CATAPULT"

- ❏ When the Dolphins beat the Steelers, the victory **CATAPULTED** them into first place.

- ❏ The Atlas entry won at Indianapolis by drafting behind the lead car and **CATAPULTING** forward to take the lead at the finish line.

- ❏ Before the invention of cannons, **CATAPULTS** were used by armies to attack castles and forts.

Match the word with its definition.

___	1. **bulwark**	a. to criticize harshly
___	2. **cache**	b. to throw or launch
___	3. **cacophony**	c. harsh sounds
___	4. **cajole**	d. immature and inexperienced
___	5. **callous**	e. unfeeling, insensitive
___	6. **callow**	f. a defensive wall
___	7. **candor**	g. to wheedle, coax, or persuade
___	8. **capacious**	h. a hiding place
___	9. **castigate**	i. roomy, able to hold much
___	10. **catapult**	j. truthfulness, sincere honesty

Fill in the blanks with the most appropriate word. The word form may need changing.

1. The old castle has a _____ dining room large enough to seat a small army.

2. The _____ boater did not have a life preserver, paddle, or radio onboard his sailboat.

3. Jeannie always sweet-talked and _____ her parents into letting her have her way.

4. Jimmy's mother _____ him for tracking mud on their new living room carpet.

5. The police uncovered a _____ of weapons and money at the gang's hideout.

6. Without regard to feelings, our teacher said she would criticize our term papers with absolute _____.

7. An unpleasant _____ of sound was produced as the orchestra tuned their instruments. But once they began to play together the sounds became euphonious.

8. When the Dolphins beat the Steelers, the victory _____ them into first place.

9. The _____ movie star would not sign autographs or even acknowledge her fans.

10. Quebec City is the only city in North America with a _____ built entirely around it.

CATHARSIS
(kuh THAR sis) *n.*
an emotional or psychological
cleansing that brings relief or renewal

Link: **CATS AND HORSES**

"CAT AND HORSE CATHARSIS"

❑ Psychologists now know that the companionship
of domesticated pets can lead to a **CATHARSIS**
for mentally disturbed patients.

❑ After Jeremy returned to the French World War II
battlefield he had known fifty years before, he said
he found the experience **CATHARTIC**.

❑ Getting out of the city and going to the mountains
is Chuck's annual **CATHARSIS**.

CAUCUS
(KAW kus) *n./v.*
a meeting of the members of a political party to make decisions; to assemble in or hold a caucus

Link: **CACTUS**

"A CACTUS CAUCUS"

- ❏ A **CAUCUS** was held by the members of the delegation to determine if they should hold a special **CAUCUS** for the unmarried members.

- ❏ Some delegates to political conventions are selected in **CAUCUSES**, while others are appointed.

- ❏ During the monthly **CAUCUS**, the senator from Florida brought up the issue of runaway insurance rate hikes.

CEREBRAL
(suh REE brul) *adj.*
of or relating to the brain;
an intellectual person

Link: **CEREAL**

*"Eat your **CEREAL** so you'll grow up
and be **CEREBRAL** like your father."*

- ❏ **CEREBRAL** for a football player, the wily Kansas quarterback rarely called a play that wasn't well planned and thought out.

- ❏ Dr. Clark was too **CEREBRAL** to be a boy scout leader. Instead of saying "pitch your tents over by the cliff," he would confuse everyone with his big words and say, "construct the canvas shelters in the proximity of the promontory."

- ❏ The **CEREBRAL** young man received a perfect score on his SAT test.

CERTIFY

(SUR tuh fie) *v.*
to confirm formally; verify

Link: **HURT A FLY**

*"George Washington never told a lie, and he would **CERTIFY** that he never **HURT A FLY**."*

- ❏ The valuable papers arrived by **CERTIFIED** mail.
- ❏ In front of the entire commission, Jane was asked to **CERTIFY** she could prove her accusations.
- ❏ Jack was a **CERTIFIABLE** liar and crook, wanted in many countries by the authorities.

CHASM

(KAZ um) *n.*
a deep opening in the earth's surface; a gorge;
differences of opinion, interests, loyalties

Link: **SPASM**

*"A **SPASM** above the **CHASM**"*

- ❑ "There are **CHASMS** and there are **CHASMS**," said the professor. "The Grand Canyon is one big **CHASM**, but I fear some of you have **CHASMS** between your ears."

- ❑ There was a **CHASM** of difference between their attitudes of what a marriage should consist of.

- ❑ We crossed the huge **CHASM** on a flimsy rope bridge.

CHATTEL
(CHAT ul)
an item of personal,
movable property; slave

Link: **CATTLE**

*"Tex's **CATTLE** were his **CHATTEL**."*

❑ The bank held a **CHATTEL** mortgage on all our office equipment, chairs, computers, and even our electric clock.

❑ Please do not order me around, Lady Boswell, I am neither your servant nor your **CHATTEL**.

❑ The **CHATTEL** belonging to Herodotos of Athens at his death were sixteen slaves, seven horses, six hunting dogs, and three dwarf gladiators.

CHIDE

(chide) *v.*
to scold; to voice disapproval

Link: **LIED**

*"The good fairy CHIDED
Pinocchio because he LIED."*

❑ When Bobby threw his toys against the wall, his father **CHIDED** him for his bad temper.

❑ I don't mind being **CHIDED** for things I did, but I hate being **CHIDED** for what my sneaky sister Elizabeth did.

❑ The sergeant told the private that he was going to **CHIDE** him each time he didn't properly clean his rifle.

CHRONIC
(KRAHN ik) *adj.*
continuing for a long time; continuous

Link: **RON'S HIC**

"RON'S HICcups were CHRONIC."

- ❑ George was a **CHRONIC** complainer, he never saw the positive side of anything.

- ❑ When lower back pain becomes **CHRONIC**, it's time to see a doctor.

- ❑ Her **CHRONIC** gossiping led to her being kicked out of the garden club.

CIRCA

(SUR ka) *n.*
about; at an estimated
historical time period

Link: **CIRCUS**

*"The first known **CIRCUS** took place **CIRCA** 200,000 BC."*

❑ The exact date of the first Egyptian dynasty is not known, but it is believed to have occurred **CIRCA** 3000 BC.

❑ **CIRCA** is another word for "about" or "more or less," and always refers to a passage of time.

❑ John is an expert on weapons produced **CIRCA** 1800.

CITADEL
(SIT uh dl) *n.*
a fortress overlooking
a city; a stronghold

Link: **SIT WELL**

*"It pays to **SIT WELL** on
the edge of a **CITADEL**."*

❏ Charlie was a **CITADEL** of strength, always there
for you no matter what.

❏ West Point is considered a **CITADEL** of military
learning, a fact easily understood when you come
to understand that most generals attended West
Point.

❏ There are many ancient **CITADELS** in Spain; they
are among the attractions most visited by tourists.

VOCABULARY CARTOONS Review #7

Match the word with its definition.

___ 1. **catharsis**
___ 2. **caucus**
___ 3. **cerebral**
___ 4. **certify**
___ 5. **chasm**
___ 6. **chattel**
___ 7. **chide**
___ 8. **chronic**
___ 9. **circa**
___ 10. **citadel**

a. personal property; slave
b. to confirm formally; verify
c. a meeting of a political party
d. continuing for a long time
e. of or relating to the brain
f. a fortress overlooking a city
g. at an estimated historical time
h. to scold; to voice disapproval
i. an opening in the earth's surface
j. an emotional or psychological cleansing that brings relief

Fill in the blanks with the most appropriate word. The word form may need changing.

1. The _____ young man received a perfect score on his SAT test.

2. When lower back pain becomes _____, it's time to see a doctor.

3. Getting out of the city and going to the mountains is Chuck's annual _____.

4. The _____ belonging to Herodotos of Athens at his death were sixteen slaves, seven horses, six hunting dogs, and three dwarf gladiators.

5. When Bobby threw his toys against the wall, his father _____ him for his bad temper.

6. During the monthly _____, the senator from Florida brought up the issue of runaway insurance rate hikes.

7. The exact date of the first Egyptian dynasty is not known, but it is believed to have occurred _____ 3000 BC.

8. The valuable papers arrived by _____ mail.

9. There are many ancient _____ in Spain; they are among the attractions most visited by tourists.

10. We crossed the huge _____ on a flimsy rope bridge.

CLAIMANT
(KLAY munt) *n.*
a person making a claim

Link: **CLAIM ANT**

THEY'RE MINE!

"A CLAIMANT CLAIMING ANTS"

- ❑ The **CLAIMANT** of the Virginia City silver mine was Scott "Wormy" McClennahan, a miner.

- ❑ The judge awarded all six of the **CLAIMANTS** an equal share of the insurance money.

- ❑ Rosalie not only wanted the house in her divorce from Robert, but she was also the **CLAIMANT** of his art collection.

CLOISTER
(KLOY stur) *n.*
a tranquil, secluded place

Link: **OYSTER**

*"An **OYSTER** in his **CLOISTER**"*

❑ Mary regarded her sewing room as a **CLOISTER** where she could withdraw from her hectic life as a mother of six and enjoy moments of privacy.

❑ (To **CLOISTER** someone is to place them in a place of seclusion, although they may or may not be in the company of others.) Jim **CLOISTERED** himself in his hotel room for the entire week of his vacation.

COMMODIOUS
(kuh MOH dee us) *adj.*
spacious, roomy, capacious

Link: **COMMODE**

*"A **COMMODIOUS COMMODE**"*

❑ The rooms in the castle were so **COMMODIOUS** that they were as large as the average home.

❑ The **COMMODIOUS** limousine accommodated the entire family and our luggage.

❑ In Hong Kong, the government has built several million apartments for the working class in recent decades. Compared to western standards, they are not very **COMMODIOUS**, only about half the size of a small, two-bedroom apartment in the United States.

COMPRISE
(kum PRIZE) *v.*
to consist of; to include, to
contain, to be made up of

Link: **SURPRISE**

*"It was not a pleasant **SURPRISE** when
the pirates discovered their treasure was
COMPRISED only of party favors."*

❏ If we had one more kitten in the house, the litter
would **COMPRISE** thirteen.

❏ A basketball team **COMPRISES** five players and
any number of substitutes the coach wants to
allow on the team.

❏ The first aid kit was **COMPRISED** of a bottle of
aspirin, two gauze pads, and a pair of scissors.

CONGENIAL

(kun JEEN ee ul) *adj.*
pleasant to be around;
social, agreeable

Link: **JEANS**

"Folks in JEANS are very CONGENIAL."

❑ The **CONGENIAL** Dr. Armstrong always had a smile and a kind word for his patients, and candies for the children.

❑ Miss Florida was voted Miss **CONGENIALITY** in the Miss America pageant.

❑ The atmosphere at the property appraiser's office is **CONGENIAL**. Everyone enjoys their job, and visitors are welcome at any time.

CONNOISSEUR
(kahn uh SUR) *n.*
an expert, particularly in
matters of art and taste

Link: **KING OF SEWER**

*"The **KING OF the SEWER** is a **CONNOISSEUR** of garbage."*

❑ My uncle is a **CONNOISSEUR** of fine wines.

❑ Art dealer, Jorge Guizar, is a **CONNOISSEUR** of Mexican art of the 19th century.

❑ When it came to coins, Jerry proclaimed he was a **CONNOISSEUR**, because he had collected them all his life.

CONSENSUS

(kun SEN sus) *n.*
general agreement

Link: **SENDS US**

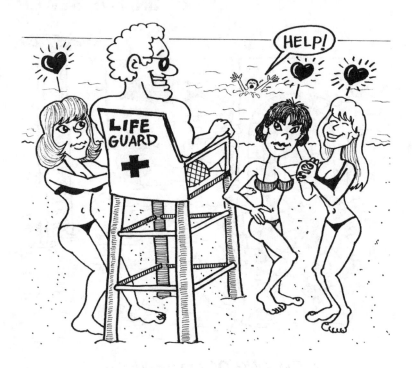

"We are in CONSENSUS, this guy SENDS US."

- ❑ The family **CONSENSUS** was to celebrate Christmas at Aunt Karen's house this year.

- ❑ The **CONSENSUS** of the faculty was that no more chili dogs were to be served at the school lunch.

- ❑ A **CONSENSUS** is more than a majority, it means most everyone agrees.

COTERIE
(KOH tuh ree) *n.*
a circle of close associates or friends

Link: **COAT FOR THREE**

*"The maestro and his **COTERIE**
in a **COAT FOR THREE**"*

- ❑ Today's tennis stars rarely travel alone, but with a **COTERIE** of managers and coaches.

- ❑ Rock stars have a **COTERIE** of fans who follow them around like leeches.

- ❑ You have to be a member of Daisy's **COTERIE**, or you don't count at all, in the opinion of Daisy.

COUNTENANCE
(KOWN tuh nunz) *n.*
a person's face, especially the expression

Link: **COUNT THE NUTS**

*"By their facial **COUNTENANCE** alone
it was easy to **COUNT THE NUTS**."*

- ❑ The submarine commander's **COUNTENANCE** belied his true feelings of anxiety and fear.

- ❑ John Barrymore had a magnificent series of **COUNTENANCES**, one for every role he played.

- ❑ (To **COUNTENANCE** something is to tolerate or approve of it.) The coach **COUNTENANCED** the players' horse play, even though he didn't approve of it.

COUP
(koo) *n.*
the violent overthrow of a government by a small group; a victorious accomplishment

Link: **CREW**

*"In a midnight **COUP**, the mutinous **CREW** of 'The Bounty' threw Captain Bligh off his ship."*

❑ In this century alone there have been almost one hundred military **COUPS** in Latin America.

❑ It was a real **COUP** for James when his teammates elected him captain of the basketball team.

❑ The violent **COUP** ended when the radical political leaders were escorted out of the capitol in shackles.

Match the word with its definition.

___ 1. **claimant**
___ 2. **cloister**
___ 3. **commodious**
___ 4. **comprise**
___ 5. **congenial**
___ 6. **connoisseur**
___ 7. **consensus**
___ 8. **coterie**
___ 9. **countenance**
___ 10. **coup**

a. a person's facial expression
b. general agreement
c. a circle of close friends
d. spacious, roomy, capacious
e. the overthrow of a government
f. to contain, to be made up of
g. pleasant to be around
h. a tranquil, secluded place
i. a person making a claim
j. an expert

Fill in the blanks with the most appropriate word.
The word form may need changing.

1. The _____ limousine accommodated the entire family and our luggage.

2. The judge awarded all six of the _____ an equal share of the insurance money.

3. The first aid kit was _____ of a bottle of aspirin, two gauze pads, and a pair of scissors.

4. The family _____ was to celebrate Christmas at Aunt Karen's house this year.

5. The _____ Dr. Armstrong always had a smile and a kind word for his patients, and candies for the children.

6. Rock stars have a _____ of fans who follow them around like leeches.

7. The submarine commander's _____ belied his true feelings of anxiety and fear.

8. The violent _____ ended when the radical political leaders were escorted out of the capitol in shackles.

9. Mary regarded her sewing room as a _____ where she could withdraw from her hectic life as a mother of six and enjoy moments of privacy.

10. My uncle is a _____ of fine wines.

COUTURE
(kuh TOUR) *n.*
fashion designers; clothes
created by fashion designers

Link: **FUTURE**

*"That's what we'll be wearing,
the **COUTURE** of the **FUTURE**."*

- ❏ Jane works for a department store chain and they sent her to Paris to study the latest **COUTURE**.

- ❏ Henry studied the art of **COUTURIER** for three years in the finest French design institutions.

- ❏ The fashion model walked the runway wearing the latest **COUTURE**.

COWER
(KOW ur) *v.*
to cringe in fear; to shrink away

Link: **COW**

*"Bessie, the **COWERING COW**, never could stand the sight of her own milk."*

❑ When Sheriff Wild Bill Hickok entered the Last Chance Saloon, the villains **COWERED** in fear.

❑ The sound of the rusty door opening in the middle of the night made Sue **COWER** under her sheets.

❑ Jack **COWERED** in frustration just to think about coming home from vacation and finding all the homework he had to catch up on.

CRANNY
(KRAN ee) *n.*
a small opening as in a wall or rock face

Link: **GRANNY**

*"**GRANNY** got stuck in the **CRANNY**."*

- ❏ The secret message was found stuffed into a small **CRANNY** in the courtyard wall next to the church.

- ❏ Rock climbers look for any **CRANNY** where they can get a secure foothold.

- ❏ We searched the house from top to bottom and never overlooked a single nook or **CRANNY**.

CRAVEN
(KRAY ven) *adj.*
lacking the least bit of courage;
cowardly

Link: **RAVEN**

"A CRAVEN RAVEN on the run"

- ❑ The soldier was full of bluster about how bravely he would fight, but his comrades later found him to be **CRAVEN** once the battle started.

- ❑ To let his wife do his fighting for him was the act of a **CRAVEN** husband with no backbone.

- ❑ The **CRAVENLY** act of the assassin, John Wilkes Booth, led to the death of President Lincoln.

CREDITOR
(KRED ih ter) *n.*
a person or entity to whom money is owed

Link: **PREDATOR**

*"Beware the **CREDITOR** who is a **PREDATOR**."*

❑ Mr. Randolph's lawyer recommended he declare bankruptcy; he had too many **CREDITORS** and not enough assets with which to pay.

❑ **CREDITORS** usual charge interest on the money they loan.

❑ Visa, Master Card, and American Express companies are **CREDITORS**.

CRITERION

(kry TEER ee un) *n.*
a standard or rule by which something
can be judged; a basis for judgment

Link: **LIBRARIAN**

*"A **CRITERION** for any **LIBRARIAN** is
that she must know how to read."*

- ❑ There is no special **CRITERION** for making a fortune, but some say the fastest way is to marry rich.

- ❑ (**CRITERION** is singular. **CRITERIA** is plural.) The physical **CRITERIA** for a good basketball player are to be seven feet tall and jump like a kangaroo.

- ❑ The **CRITERION** for becoming a lawyer is graduating from law school and passing the state bar exam.

CUBISM
(KYOO biz um) *n.*
a style of art in which the subject matter is
portrayed by geometric forms, especially cubes

Link: **CUBES**

*"By the look of these **CUBES**, you are
an artist of the school of **CUBISM**."*

- ❑ **CUBISM** is a style of art that stresses abstract structure at the expense of other pictorial elements by fragmenting the form of those objects that are to be depicted.

- ❑ Pablo Picasso did not originate **CUBISM**, but he is credited with popularizing it.

- ❑ By the design of the new building you can tell the architect was partial to **CUBISM**.

CURTAIL
(kur TALE) *v.*
to truncate or abridge; to lessen,
usually by cutting away from

Link: **CAT TAIL**

"Rex readies himself to
***CURTAIL** the **CAT'S TAIL**."*

❑ The chairman requested that we should **CURTAIL** any further discussion of women's rights until the women arrived.

❑ Sheriff McDougall **CURTAILED** all further night patrols east of the river until bullet-proof windows were installed in his patrol cars.

❑ Mike's knee injury **CURTAILED** his career as a professional football player.

CURVILINEAR
(kurv ah LIN ee ur) *adj.*
formed, bound, or
characterized by curved lines

Link: **CURVY LINES**

*"The skater's **CURVY LINES** outlined her
CURVILINEAR skating program."*

- ❏ Squares and rectangles have no **CURVILINEAR** lines.

- ❏ Engineers have special instruments to lay out **CURVILINEAR** streets in subdivisions.

- ❏ The **CURVILINEAR** shape of sports cars makes them more aerodynamic, which gives them less drag and allows them to travel faster.

DAMPER
(DAM pur) *n.*
one that depresses or restrains;
a dulling or deadening influence

Link: **DAMP PAW**

*"A **DAMP PAW** can put a
DAMPER on a good time."*

- ❏ The jury trial seemed to be going the way of the defense until an eyewitness put a **DAMPER** on the defendant's hopes by identifying him as the one who committed the crime.

- ❏ The family was excited about their vacation until their father put a **DAMPER** on their plans, saying he was sorry, but there was no money for a vacation this year.

- ❏ The unexpected rain put a **DAMPER** on plans to have a picnic at the beach.

VOCABULARY CARTOONS Review #9

Match the word with its definition.

___ 1. **couture**
___ 2. **cower**
___ 3. **cranny**
___ 4. **craven**
___ 5. **creditor**
___ 6. **criterion**
___ 7. **cubism**
___ 8. **curtail**
___ 9. **curvilinear**
___ 10. **damper**

a. a small opening as in a wall
b. to cringe in fear; to shrink away
c. a standard by to be judged
d. to lessen; cut away from
e. clothes created by fashion designers
f. lacking the least bit of courage
g. characterized by curved lines
h. one that depresses or restrains
i. an entity to whom money is owed
j. a style of art is portrayed by geometric forms

Fill in the blanks with the most appropriate word. The word form may need changing.

1. When Sheriff Wild Bill Hickok entered the Last Chance Saloon, the villains _____ in fear.

2. The unexpected rain put a _____ on plans to have a picnic at the beach.

3. Rock climbers look for any _____ where they can get a secure foothold.

4. Mike's knee injury _____ his career as a professional football player.

5. Pablo Picasso did not originate _____, but he is credited with popularizing it.

6. The fashion model walked the runway wearing the latest _____.

7. Engineers have special instruments to lay out _____ streets in subdivisions.

8. Visa, Master Card, and American Express companies are _____.

9. The _____ for becoming a lawyer is graduating from law school and passing the state bar exam.

10. The soldier was full of bluster about how bravely he would fight, but his comrades later found him to be _____ .

113

DAUNTLESS
(DAWNT lis) *adj.*
fearless; unintimidated

Link: **HAUNTLESS**

*"The **DAUNTLESS** ghostbusters render
a haunted house **HAUNTLESS**."*

- [ ] **DAUNTLESS** and determined, the firemen dashed through the smoke to rescue the family trapped in the fire. **UNDAUNTED** by the flames, they stayed until everyone had been rescued. (**DAUNTLESS** and **UNDAUNTED** mean the same thing.)

- [ ] The hikers were **UNDAUNTED** by the steepness of the mountain; however, they decided to turn back when a storm appeared in the distance.

- [ ] The **DAUNTLESS** soldier attacked the enemy line with no regard to the machine gun fire and mortar rounds exploding all around him.

DEARTH
(durth) *n.*
scarcity; lack

Link: **EARTH**

*"There is a **DEARTH** of **EARTH**
in the middle of the ocean."*

- A **DEARTH** of rain last summer led to many failed crops, especially corn and cotton in the valley.

- This Broadway season was the poorest in years. Critics say this was largely due to a **DEARTH** of good playwrights.

- There always seems to be a **DEARTH** of cookies in the cookie jar after our granddaughter's visit.

DEBACLE
(dih BAH kul) *n.*
a sudden calamitous downfall;
collapse or failure

Link: **THE BUCKLE**

*"When **THE BUCKLE** broke, Shakespeare's
Hamlet became a **DEBACLE**."*

❑ It was an absolute **DEBACLE** for Agassi as he
lost the third set without winning a single point.

❑ The bank went broke as a result of a **DEBACLE**
created by the thieving board of directors.

❑ The Watergate scandal was the **DEBACLE** of the
Nixon presidency.

DEBASE
(dih BAYS) *v.*
to lower in quality, character, or value

Link: **THE BASE**

*"Big Bertha easily **DEBASED THE BASE**."*

❏ Inflation in Brazil has **DEBASED** the value of money so much that people won't stoop to recover small coins in the street.

❏ The judge sued the newspaper for **DEBASING** his character in an article claiming he was too easy on criminals.

❏ Violent crime in America **DEBASES** our country.

DECREE
(dih KREE) *n.*
an order having the force of law

Link: **SET FREE**

*"The governor **DECREED** that
all the prisoners be **SET FREE**."*

❏ The **DECREE** by the city council that all dogs
must be kept on a leash set off a bitter conflict
among dog owners.

❏ In Dodge City, during the days of the great cattle
drives of the 1880s, Sheriff Wyatt Earp enforced
the **DECREE** that all guns must be turned over to
the sheriff's deputies before a man could ride into
town.

❏ Avid smokers protested the **DECREE** which
prohibits smoking in all restaurants and public
buildings.

DEDUCE

(dee DOOS) *v.*
to come to a conclusion by
reasoning from the evidence

Link: **MOOSE**

*"Marvin the **MOOSE** wondered why Elsie the cow couldn't **DEDUCE** that he was a **MOOSE**."*

❑ When the doors to the living room were locked the day before Christmas, Peggy **DEDUCED** her mother was wrapping presents and didn't want to be disturbed.

❑ From the footprints in the snow, we **DEDUCED** that the missing hikers had wandered in circles several days before disappearing entirely.

❑ The detective **DEDUCED** that the killer's weapon was a knife based on the wounds left on the victim.

DEFAME

(dih FAYM) *v.*
to libel or slander; take away a good name

Link: **RENAME**

"When the good name of William Bonney was
DEFAMED, *reporters* ***RENAMED*** *him 'Billy the Kid'."*

❑ **DEFAMED** and defeated, Napoleon was exiled to the Island of Elba.

❑ False accusations by lying men have **DEFAMED** the reputations of many reputable woman.

❑ Thomas Jefferson was once quoted as saying, "**DEFAMATION** is becoming a way of life insomuch that a dish of tea cannot be digested without the stimulant."

Link: **DEAF**

*"The **DEAF** are **DEFT** at reading lips."*

❑ The quarterback **DEFTLY** avoided the linebacker's rush while calmly throwing a touchdown pass.

❑ In one **DEFT** move, the policeman subdued the thief and took him to the ground.

❑ The magician was so **DEFT** with a pack of cards that he could deal off the bottom with everyone watching, and no one was the wiser.

DEMAGOGUE
(DEM uh gawg) *n.*
a leader who obtains power by appealing to the emotions and prejudices of the people

Link: **THEM DOGS**

*"**THEM DOGS**, Hitler and Mussolini, were infamous **DEMAGOGUES**."*

- ❏ Historians will almost exclusively agree that Hitler and Mussolini were **DEMAGOGUES** who were greatly responsible for starting World War II. (**DEMAGOGUES** are leaders, but not in a positive way.)

- ❏ Lawyers, politicians, and other authority figures who inflame the populace to further their own aims are said to be **DEMAGOGUES** who engage in **DEMAGOGUERY**.

DEMONIC
(dee MON ik) *adj.*
one who works devilishly (a demon for work),
having a persistent force or drive; fiendish

Link: **DEMON**

*"Professor Luke E. Fer was a **DEMONIC**
DEMON when it came time for his final exams."*

❑ Walter had a **DEMONIC** approach to business;
he was only out there for himself and the money.

❑ In pursuit of an Olympic medal, Jack's practice
habits were **DEMONIC**; six hours a day on the
track was his norm.

❑ To have a **DEMONIC** attitude in attempting to
achieve your goals will sooner or later payoff.

VOCABULARY CARTOONS Review #10

Match the word with its definition.

___ 1. **dauntless**
___ 2. **dearth**
___ 3. **debacle**
___ 4. **debase**
___ 5. **decree**
___ 6. **deduce**
___ 7. **defame**
___ 8. **deft**
___ 9. **demagogue**
___ 10. **demonic**

a. a sudden downfall
b. an evil leader
c. having a persistent force or drive
d. an order having the force of law
e. fearless; unintimidated
f. skillful, dexterous
g. scarcity; lack
h. to lower in quality
i. to take away a good name
j. to come to a conclusion by reasoning from the evidence

Fill in the blanks with the most appropriate word. The word form may need changing.

1. In one _____ move, the policeman subdued the thief and took him to the ground.

2. The _____ soldier attacked the enemy line with no regard to the machine gun fire and mortar rounds exploding all around him.

3. Walter had a _____ approach to business; he was only out there for himself and the money.

4. A _____ of rain last summer led to many failed crops, especially corn and cotton in the valley.

5. Avid smokers protested the _____ which prohibits smoking in all restaurants and public buildings.

6. Historians will almost exclusively agree that Hitler and Mussolini were _____ who were greatly responsible for starting World War II.

7. False accusations by lying men have _____ the reputations of many reputable woman.

8. Inflation in Brazil has _____ the value of money so much that people won't stoop to recover small coins in the street.

9. It was an absolute _____ for Agassi as he lost the third set without winning a single point.

10. The detective _____ that the killer's weapon was a knife based on the wounds left on the victim.

124

DEMUR
(dih MYOOR) *v.*
to object, to make exception

Link: **PURE**

*"Cinderella was so **PURE** she **DEMURRED**
from drinking even a root beer."*

- ❑ Billy **DEMURRED** when his friends wanted him to run for class president.

- ❑ The mayor said he would **DEMUR** if asked to speak at the town rally.

- ❑ Nancy **DEMURRED** when Henry suggested she should share her lunch with him and his six friends.

DENOUNCE
(duh NOWNS) *v.*
to condemn; to expose critically

Link: **BOUNCE**

*"The other kangaroos **DENOUNCED** poor Roger when he was unable to **BOUNCE**."*

❏ At the press conference, the irate coach **DENOUNCED** the referees for all the bad calls he thought he had received.

❏ The captured soldiers were asked to **DENOUNCE** their government and join in the revolution of the people.

❏ The world was flabbergasted with the Russian government's **DENUNCIATION** of Stalin so soon after he died.

DESICCATE
(DES uh kayt) *v.*
to dry out completely; dehydrate

Link: **THIS DRY CAKE**

"THIS DRY CAKE has DESICCATED."

- ❑ The drought was the worst in fifty years, and the oranges on the trees were **DESICCATED**.

- ❑ The whale carcasses cast upon the beach had begun to **DESICCATE** by the time the marine biologist arrived at the scene.

- ❑ Raisins are grapes that have been shrunk and dried through a process of **DESICCATION**.

DILEMMA
(duh LEM ma) *n.*
a difficult situation where one must choose between two or more choices that seem unfavorable; any problem or predicament

Link: **LIMB**

*"The **DILEMMA** facing Jake was to go over the waterfall or to grab the **LIMB**."*

❑ John faced the **DILEMMA** of either taking a cut in pay or losing his job.

❑ Helen was on "the horns of a **DILEMMA**." She had to move with her family to another town and lose a semester in school or stay by herself until summer.

❑ It was a small **DILEMMA**, but Bill couldn't choose between pecan or cherry pie for dessert.

DISPARAGE
(dis PEAR ij) *v.*
to belittle, say uncomplimentary
things; to put down

Link: **CARRIAGE**

*"The mean stepmother **DISPARAGED**
Cinderella's **CARRIAGE**."*

- Pete was told his behavior would **DISPARAGE** the whole team's efforts.

- Robert **DISPARAGES** the accomplishments of his fellow students.

- Jealousy made Ellen make many **DISPARAG-ING** remarks about Rachel's prom dress.

DISPEL
(dis PELL) *v.*
to drive away; to dissipate

Link: **SPELL**

"The princess kissed many toads before she could DISPEL the witch's SPELL on the prince."

❏ After the crowd had been **DISPELLED** from the scene of the accident, the wreckers hauled away the tangled, wrecked automobiles.

❏ The professor told his student he wanted to **DISPEL** any thoughts she might have of receiving a better grade than she deserved just because he was a good friend of the family.

❏ My parents told us to **DISPLEL** any notions of inviting a bunch of friends over to the house and having a wild party while they were gone for the weekend.

DISPERSE
(dis PURS) *v.*
to scatter in various
directions; distribute widely

Link: **PURSE**

*"When the thug grabbed Dee's **PURSE**,
all its contents were **DISPERSED**."*

- ☐ Bonaparte **DISPERSED** his troops strategically all along the mountain's ridge where they could fire down upon the advancing Austrian Army.

- ☐ The police arrived to **DISPERSED** the raging crowd with threats of arrest if they did not leave the parade grounds.

- ☐ The investors expected that the funds would be **DISPERSED** the same day of the closing.

DISSOLUTION

(dis uh LOO shun) *n.*
the breaking up into parts; termination
of a legal bond or contract

Link: **SOLUTION**

*"When the heirs to the estate were unable to agree
on **DISSOLUTION** of their parents' home, the judge's
SOLUTION was to divide it into equal parts."*

❑ The **DISSOLUTION** of their marriage was caused
by Stan's infidelity.

❑ The **DISSOLUTION** of the committee for fine arts
left the matter of payment to the artists undecided.

❑ Nothing could prevent the **DISSOLUTION** of our
fraternity, even if we were the worst on campus.

DIVINE
(di VYNE) *v.*
to foretell a prophecy; to infer, to guess

Link: **VINE**

*"How was Tarzan to **DIVINE** this was
the time his **VINE** would break?"*

- ❑ Stockbrokers make their living helping their clients **DIVINE** when to buy and when to sell stocks.

- ❑ When you have been a policeman for years, you can almost **DIVINE** when your prisoner is telling the truth as opposed to when he is lying.

- ❑ (**DIVINE** also means supremely pleasing.) It was a **DIVINE** party, and a great time was had by all.

DOCILE

(DAHS ul) *adj.*
easily taught or controlled;
obedient, easy to handle

Link: **FOSSIL**

"A DOCILE FOSSIL"

- ❑ A desirable quality of basset hounds is that they are **DOCILE**, and that is why they are sought after as house pets.

- ❑ Cameron was a fierce competitor on the football field, but his wife said he was a sweet, **DOCILE** husband.

- ❑ The **DOCILE** dolphin was easily approached by its new trainer.

VOCABULARY CARTOONS Review #11

Match the word with its definition.

__	1. demur	a. to dry out completely; dehydrate
__	2. denounce	b. to object, to make exception
__	3. desiccate	c. to drive away; to dissipate
__	4. dilemma	d. the breaking up into parts
__	5. disparage	e. to belittle; to put down
__	6. dispel	f. easy to handle
__	7. disperse	g. a difficult situation
__	8. dissolution	h. to scatter in various directions
__	9. divine	i. to condemn; to expose critically
__	10. docile	j. to foretell a prophecy; to guess

Fill in the blanks with the most appropriate word. The word form may need changing.

1. The drought was the worst in fifty years, and the oranges on the trees were _____.

2. The _____ of their marriage was caused by Stan's infidelity.

3. The police arrived to _____ the raging crowd with threats of arrest if they did not leave the parade grounds.

4. At the press conference, the irate coach _____ the referees for all the bad calls he thought he received.

5. Jealousy made Ellen make many _____ remarks about Rachel's prom dress.

6. My parents told us to _____ any notions of inviting a bunch of friends over to the house and having a wild party while they were gone for the weekend.

7. John faced the _____ of either taking a cut in pay or losing his job.

8. The _____ dolphin was easily approached by its new trainer.

9. Stockbrokers make their living helping their clients _____ when to buy and when to sell stocks.

10. The mayor said he would _____ if asked to speak at the town rally.

135

DOLDRUMS

(DOHL drums) *n.*
a period or condition of depression or inactivity; a part of the ocean near the equator abounding in calms and squalls

Link: **DOLL DRUMS**

*"All covered with dust, the **DOLL DRUMS** were in the **DOLDRUMS**."*

❑ Ever since Jackie's dog died, he hasn't touched his toys and he mopes around day after day in the **DOLDRUMS**.

❑ Ever since the company sales have been in the **DOLDRUMS** the boss has had to layoff three salesmen.

❑ For thirteen days we were becalmed in the Horse Latitudes near the equator, our ship drifting in the **DOLDRUMS** without the faintest breeze to fill the sails of our vessel.

DOMAIN
(doe MAYN) *n.*
a territory over which one rules,
has influence or powers

Link: **PLAIN**

*"Lions have **DOMAIN** over the **PLAINS** of Africa."*

- ❑ When Minnesota Fats entered a pool hall, all the other players respectfully stopped their own games to watch him, for they knew this was his **DOMAIN**.

- ❑ The **DOMAIN** of the native Florida panther is in the Everglades and South Central Florida.

- ❑ The courtroom is the **DOMAIN** of attorneys and judges.

DORMANT

(DOR munt) *adj.*
asleep or inactive

Link: **DOOR MAT**

*"Boys! Boys! Fido may be **DORMANT**,
but he is not a **DOOR MAT**."*

- ❑ Bears hibernate in caves and remain **DORMANT** throughout the winter.

- ❑ Jim's talent for playing the French horn had been **DORMANT** for so long he lost his ability to play.

- ❑ The rain fell steadily over the **DORMANT** village as nightfall approached.

DRACONIAN
(drah KOH nee un) *adj.*
hard, severe, cruel

Link: **DRACULA**

*"Count **DRACULA** often behaved
in a **DRACONIAN** manner."*

❑ Our **DRACONIAN** professor always gives us at least three hours of homework a night and term papers to write over every holiday.

❑ Judge McNamara handed down a **DRACONIAN** sentence to the defendant: sixty days for littering.

❑ The word **DRACONIAN** did not originate with the fictional character, Count Dracula, but with an ancient Greek official named Draco who created a harsh code of laws.

DROMEDARY
(DROM ih der ee) *n.*
a one-humped domesticated camel

Link: **ROAMING DAIRY**

"On the Arabian deserts, a mother
***DROMEDARY** is a **ROAMING DAIRY**."*

❑ The **DROMEDARY** is widely used as a beast of
burden in Northern Africa and Western Asia.

❑ A **DROMEDARY** is also known as an Arabian
camel.

❑ The highlight of our trip to Egypt was riding
DROMEDARIES around the Great Pyramids of
Giza.

DULCET

(DULL set) *adj.*
melodious, soft, soothing;
pleasing to the ear

Link: **DULL SIT**

*"If you don't like opera, even the most **DULCET** tones of the finest sopranos make for a **DULL SIT**."*

❑ Senator Kramer was a political campaigner who could hypnotize an audience with sweet words and **DULCET** tones.

❑ Jeff's parents declared there was nothing **DULCET** about the rock-and-roll music that shook the house from his room every morning as he dressed for school.

❑ The **DULCET** music in the elevator made the ride to the fifty-fifth floor pleasurable.

DURESS
(dyoo RES) *n.*
hardship, restraint, confinement

Link: **CONFESS**

*"During interrogation, the suspect was
under DURESS to CONFESS."*

- ❑ The judge ruled the defendant was under
  DURESS when the police got his confession, and
  therefore his confession could not be used as
  evidence.

- ❑ It is only in recent years that social scientists have
  come to understand that many people laboring in
  competitive industries are under career **DURESS**.

- ❑ The crew was under **DURESS** after drifting for
  three days in a rubber raft with no food or water.

EDIFICE

(ED uh fis) *n.*
a building, especially one of
imposing appearance or size

Link: **ATE A FACE**

HE ONLY EATS THE FINEST BUILDINGS!

*"The Great Kong **ATE** the north
FACE of the **EDIFICE**."*

❏ The construction of one **EDIFICE** led to another,
and New York City became a skyline of enormous
skyscrapers.

❏ The Taj Mahal may not be the largest **EDIFICE**
ever constructed, but surely it is one of the most
imposing in the world.

❏ Neither imposing in appearance or size, you could
hardly refer to an outhouse as an **EDIFICE**.

EFFACE
(uh FACE) *v.*
to rub away

Link: **ERASE**

*"How to **EFFACE** a face by **ERASING** it"*

❏ We came upon a cemetery by the sea. Many of the headstone inscriptions had been **EFFACED** by the ravages of time, but we could make out many that were well over two hundred years old.

❏ To assure that he left no clues, the thief **EFFACED** his fingerprints from the stolen car.

❏ It was hard to make out the old coin's date because it had been **EFFACED** over time.

EGALITARIAN
(ih gal uh TARE ee un) *adj.*
advocating the doctrine of equal
rights for all citizens

Link: **THE GAL I'M MARRYIN'**

*"THE GAL I'M MARRYIN' is
an EGALITARIAN."*

❑ The Communists preached an **EGALITARIAN**
philosophy, but in the end they were the same old
fascists the world has known through the ages.

❑ The founders of the Declaration of Independence
were no better; they also preached **EGALITARIAN**
principles, yet at the same time they owned slaves.

❑ Martin Luther King was a true **EGALITARIAN**, he
preached for equal rights for all citizens.

Match the word with its definition.

__	1. doldrums	a.	a one-humped domesticated camel
__	2. domain	b.	a period of depression or inactivity
__	3. dormant	c.	to rub away
__	4. draconian	d.	advocating the doctrine of equal rights
__	5. dromedary	e.	melodious, soft, soothing
__	6. dulcet	f.	a territory over which one rules
__	7. duress	g.	hard, severe, cruel
__	8. edifice	h.	asleep or inactive
__	9. efface	i.	an imposing building
__	10. egalitarian	j.	hardship, restraint, confinement

Fill in the blanks with the most appropriate word. The word form may need changing.

1. The crew was under _____ after drifting for three days in a rubber raft with no food or water.

2. The _____ of the native Florida panther is in the Everglades and South Central Florida.

3. Ever since Jackie's dog died, he hasn't touched his toys and he mopes around day after day in the _____.

4. The _____ music in the elevator made the ride to the fifty-fifth floor pleasurable.

5. Bears hibernate in caves and remain _____ throughout the winter.

6. It was hard to make out the old coin's date because it had been _____ over time.

7. Martin Luther King was a true _____, he preached for equal rights for all citizens.

8. The construction of one _____ led to another, and New York City became a skyline of enormous skyscrapers.

9. The highlight of our trip to Egypt was riding _____ around the Great Pyramids of Giza.

10. Our _____ professor always gives us at least three hours of homework a night and term papers to write over every holiday.

ELAPSE
(ee LAPS) *v.*
to pass or go by (said of time)

Link: **COLLAPSE**

*"Ted ran the mile in the **ELAPSED** time of three minutes, forty-seven seconds, and then **COLLAPSED**."*

- Time **ELAPSES** slowly when someone is waiting for important news.

- Two years **ELAPSED** before they were to meet again, but all the time Jonathan knew Annette was the girl he was going to marry.

- During World War II, the siege of Stalingrad lasted five months; in the **ELAPSING** battle 750,000 Russians and 400,000 Germans died.

ELFIN
(EL fin) *adj.*
small and sprightly;
mischievous, fairylike

Link: **ELEPHANT**

*"An **ELFIN ELEPHANT** is
a strange sight to see."*

❑ Jane is very small and has a magical **ELFIN**
   charm about her until she starts to sing. Then she
   sounds like a bullfrog in a pond.

❑ The entire family had an **ELFIN** quality, like little
   people who belonged in the Land of Lilliputians.

❑ The **ELFIN** character of Tinkerbell in the Walt
   Disney movie *Peter Pan* will always be
   remembered by generations of Disney fans.

EMBELLISH
(im BEL ish) *v.*
to beautify by adding ornaments; to
add fanciful or fictitious details to

Link: **BELLY**

*"**BELLY** dancers **EMBELLISH** their
BELLY buttons with jewels."*

❑ Eric **EMBELLISHED** his fishing stories; you would
think his catches were as big as whales.

❑ A little **EMBELLISHMENT** to a story rarely hurts,
and makes the telling more engaging.

❑ Rod was eliminated as a job prospect when the
prospective employer learned he **EMBELLISHED**
his educational background to include a college
degree he did not possess.

EMBODY
(em BAH dee) *v.*
to give bodily form to; to personify;
to make part of a system

Link: **BODY**

*"Jimmy sculpted a statue with the likeness of his face,
but which **EMBODIED** a **BODY** he'd never possess."*

❏ Virginia Satir was a wonderful therapist who
EMBODIED in her own life the loving principles
she taught to her students.

❏ The **EMBODIMENT** of universal human values is
to be found in the Boy Scouts Oath every scout
must take to become a member.

❏ Bob was a perfect candidate for school president
because he **EMBODIED** the issues and feelings
of the student body.

EMIT

(ee MIT) *v.*
to send or give out; to express, utter

Link: **SPIT**

*"Uncle Otto sure could **EMIT** a
lot of chewing tobacco **SPIT**."*

- ❏ The new federal laws on automobile **EMISSIONS** are directed at reducing pollution on our nation's highways.

- ❏ The sleeping dog **EMITTED** a groan which startled us.

- ❏ David told the mechanic that the car **EMITTED** a strange sound when he started the engine.

EMULATE

(EM yuh late) *v.*
to attempt to equal or surpass;
especially through imitation

Link: **IMITATE**

"Jimmy EMULATES his dad by IMITATING him."

❑ Most people **EMULATE** those they most admire.

❑ The famous golfer, Tiger Woods, has a golf swing that many golfers try to **EMULATE**.

❑ Pete **EMULATED** his older brother but was too small to make the baseball team.

ENDURE
(in DYOOR) *v.*
to carry on through despite
hardships; to put up with

Link: **MANURE**

*"Cowboys **ENDURE** a lot of **MANURE**."*

- ❏ Settlers in the 1800s **ENDURED** many hardships on their way to California.

- ❏ "I can't **ENDURE** the solitude," Jimbo Marks told his lawyer, as the sheriff placed him in an isolation cell awaiting trial.

- ❏ The **ENDURING** quality I recall most with loving memory about my Aunt Emma was that she never had a bad word to say about anyone.

ENGULF

(in GULF) *v.*
to surround or enclose completely

Link: **GULF**

*"The **GULF** of Mexico **ENGULFS**
many deserted islands."*

- ❏ The movie stars were **ENGULFED** by a swarm of paparazzi as they arrived at the Academy Awards ceremony.

- ❏ An **ENGULFING** movement by the Union troops cut off the Confederate retreat.

- ❏ The hurricane completely **ENGULFED** the town in a surge of wind and water.

ENRAGE
(in RAYJ) *v.*
to put in a rage; infuriate, anger

Link: **HEN CAGE**

*"An **ENRAGED** farmer discovering
a fox in the **HEN CAGE**"*

❑ What **ENRAGES** my wife is when I forget to wipe my feet before coming into the house.

❑ Muriel's boss was **ENRAGED** when he found out she had gone on her vacation to the Caribbean and left a lot of unfinished work on her desk.

❑ The crowd became **ENRAGED** when it was announced that the concert had been cancelled.

ENRAPTURE

(en RAP chur) *v.*
to delight, to thrill or give pleasure

Link: **CAPTURE**

*"The head-hunters were **ENRAPTURED** when
they **CAPTURED** Mr. and Mrs. Cranium."*

❑ John and Mary were **ENRAPTURED** when they
heard they had won a new car in the YMCA fund-
raising lottery.

❑ It was an **ENRAPTURING** performance. Everyone
was thrilled to attend the revival of Tennessee
Williams' play, *A Streetcar Named Desire.*

❑ The kids were **ENRAPTURED** with the idea of
taking the day off from school and going to Disney
World.

VOCABULARY CARTOONS Review #13

Match the word with its definition.

__ 1. elapse   a. mischievous, fairylike
__ 2. elfin   b. to pass or go by
__ 3. embellish   c. to add fanciful or fictitious details to
__ 4. embody   d. to give bodily form to; to personify
__ 5. emit   e. to put up with
__ 6. emulate   f. to put in a rage; infuriate, anger
__ 7. endure   g. to delight, to thrill or give pleasure
__ 8. engulf   h. to surround or enclose completely
__ 9. enrage   i. to attempt to equal or surpass
__ 10. enrapture   j. to send or give out

Fill in the blanks with the most appropriate word.
The word form may need changing.

1. The sleeping dog _____ a groan which startled us.

2. Settlers in the 1800s _____ many hardships on their way to California.

3. The _____ character of Tinkerbell in the Walt Disney movie *Peter Pan* will always be remembered by generations of Disney fans.

4. The hurricane completely _____ the town in a surge of wind and water.

5. Two years _____ before they were to meet again, but all the time Jonathan knew Annette was the girl he was going to marry.

6. The famous golfer, Tiger Woods, has a golf swing that many golfers try to _____.

7. The crowd became _____ when it was announced that the concert had been cancelled.

8. Eric _____ his fishing stories; you would think his catches were as big as whales.

9. The kids were _____ with the idea of taking the day off from school and going to Disney World.

10. Bob was a perfect candidate for school president because he _____ the issues and feelings of the student body.

157

ENSEMBLE

(ahn SOM bul) *n.*
a coordinated outfit or costume;
a musical group

Link: **HANDSOME DEVIL**

*"James Bond was a **HANDSOME DEVIL***
*in his spy **ENSEMBLE.***"

❏ Darla found the perfect pair of shoes to match her **ENSEMBLE** she is going to wear to the prom.

❏ A French fashion designer will work an entire year to get ready to show his **ENSEMBLES**.

❏ The wedding **ENSEMBLE** consisted of a troupe of gypsy musicians, dancers, and singers.

ENTICE
(in TICE) *v.*
to lure, to attract, to tempt
in a pleasing fashion

Link: **MICE**

*"Fido uses **MICE** to **ENTICE** cats."*

- ❏ The delicious aroma of popcorn in the theater lobby **ENTICED** us to purchase a large bucket before the movie.

- ❏ An **ENTICING** feature of working in a bakery is that you get to eat all the doughnuts you want.

- ❏ Your job proposal in Michigan is **ENTICING**, but my family likes it here in Palm Beach; Michigan's winters are too cold for native Floridians like us.

ENTOMB
(in TOOM) *v.*
to place in or as if in a tomb, or a grave

Link: **ROOM**

"Ahmed, you fool, you have
ENTOMBED *us in the burial* ***ROOM.***"

❑ The Egyptians **ENTOMBED** their kings in special burial chambers together with all their possessions needed in the afterlife.

❑ There have been cases where people, thought dead, were **ENTOMBED** while still alive.

❑ In the Pittsburgh coal mine disaster of 1938, thirty-six coal miners were **ENTOMBED** in a tunnel for thirteen days. Only fourteen survived.

ENTOMOLOGY
(en tuh MOL uh jee) *n.*
the scientific study of insects

Link: **APOLOGY**

*"An **ENTOMOLOGIST** making his
APOLOGY to the insects he must study"*

- ❑ The primary function of **ENTOMOLOGISTS** is to discover how to prevent insects from destroying crops.

- ❑ Bobby use to collect bugs when he was a kid so it didn't surprise us when he latter became an **ENTOMOLOGIST**.

- ❑ (Many words ending in **GIST** refer to a person of science in their particular field.) A **GEOLOGIST** studies the earth; a **PSYCHOLOGIST** is a scientist of human behavior; and a **METEOROLOGIST** is a person who studies the atmosphere and weather.

ENTREAT

(en TREET) *v.*
to ask earnestly; to implore, plead, beg

Link: **TREAT**

*"What is more common than a child ENTREATING
a parent for a TREAT of candy or ice cream."*

❑ Roger said he would **ENTREAT** Professor Jones
to permit us to take the exam early so we could go
on the road with the booster club.

❑ Our entire family **ENTREATED** our father to take
us on a summer vacation to Europe.

❑ The judge listened to the **ENTREATIES** of the
prisoner and decided to give him a suspended
sentence because of his family situation.

ERUDITE
(ER yoo dyte) *adj.*
deeply learned, scholarly

Link: **AIRTIGHT**

*"Knowing that his case was **AIRTIGHT**, the defense attorney became confident and **ERUDITE**."*

- ❏ Most professional speakers are **ERUDITE**, with the understanding of proper grammatical structure and a large vocabulary at their command.

- ❏ When mom was diagnosed with cancer, we searched for the most **ERUDITE** doctor we could find.

- ❏ (To be **ERUDITE** is to have **ERUDITION**.) The extent of Dr. Smith's library is an indication of his **ERUDITION**.

EUPHONIOUS
(yoo PHONE ee us)
pleasing to the ear

Link: **YOU PHONE US**

"You must be beautiful because you sound so
***EUPHONIOUS** when **YOU PHONE US**."*

- ❑ Carly sings in the choir because she has a sweet, **EUPHONIOUS** voice.

- ❑ The low, **EUPHONIOUS** croaking of the summer frogs was music to Jeff's ear.

- ❑ The grunting of a mature elephant seal is anything but **EUPHONIOUS**.

EVADE
(ee VAYD) *v.*
to elude or avoid by cunning;
to flee from a pursuer

Link: **BLADE**

"A magician's secret for EVADING BLADES"

❏ The escaped prisoners **EVADED** the authorities by breaking into a church and disguising themselves as nuns.

❏ Jane always managed to **EVADE** helping her sister wash the dinner dishes by claiming she had home-work to do.

❏ Their romance never really blossomed as their friends expected because Sarah was the pursuer, but Bill was the **EVADER**.

EVOKE
(ee VOHK) *v.*
to summon forth, call to mind,
awaken, produce, suggest

Link: **COKE**

*"Sometimes a song, a picture, even a **COKE**, can **EVOKE** the most poignant of youthful memories."*

- ❏ A clap of thunder and a flash of lightning over the old castle **EVOKED** dark spirits for the villagers who remember the night of the headless ghosts.

- ❏ The Japanese sneak attack on Pearl Harbor **EVOKED** the United States into World War II.

- ❏ Grandpa tried to **EVOKE** a smile from the baby by tickling her chin.

EXHUME
(ig ZOOM) *v.*
to dig up from a grave;
to bring to light, uncover

Link: **TOMB**

*"Archeologists like to **EXHUME TOMBS**."*

- ❏ The judge issued a court order to **EXHUME** the grave of an unknown soldier.

- ❏ Historians **EXHUMED** the literary reputation of novelist Jack London.

- ❏ Mrs. Brown **EXHUMED** old love letters sent to her by her husband before they were married.

Match the word with its definition.

___ 1. ensemble   a. to place in or as if in a tomb or grave
___ 2. entice   b. pleasing to the ear
___ 3. entomb   c. a coordinated outfit or costume
___ 4. entomology   d. deeply learned, scholarly
___ 5. entreat   e. to lure, to attract, to tempt
___ 6. erudite   f. the scientific study of insects
___ 7. euphonious   g. to ask earnestly; to implore, plead, beg
___ 8. evade   h. to elude or avoid by cunning
___ 9. evoke   i. to dig up from a grave; uncover
___ 10. exhume   j. to summon forth, call to mind, awaken

Fill in the blanks with the most appropriate word. The word form may need changing.

1. The escaped prisoners _____ the authorities by breaking into a church and disguising themselves as nuns.

2. Grandpa tried to _____ a smile from the baby by tickling her chin.

3. The delicious aroma of popcorn in the theater lobby _____ us to purchase a large bucket before the movie.

4. The judge issued a court order to _____ the grave of an unknown soldier.

5. Carly sings in the choir because she has a sweet, _____ voice.

6. When mom was diagnosed with cancer, we searched for the most _____ doctor we could find.

7. The primary function of _____ is to discover how to prevent insects from destroying crops.

8. Darla found the perfect pair of shoes to match her _____ she is going to wear to the prom.

9. Our entire family _____ our father to take us on a summer vacation to Europe.

10. The Egyptians _____ their kings in special burial chambers together with all their possessions needed in the afterlife.

EXPUNGE
(iks PUNJ) *v.*
to remove; to delete; to erase

Link: **SPONGE**

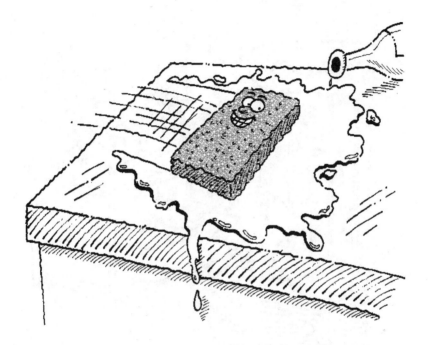

*"A **SPONGE EXPUNGING** a spill"*

- ❑ The judge ordered the clerk to **EXPUNGE** the lawyer's statement from the record.

- ❑ The wet and muddy footprints were **EXPUNGED** with soap and water.

- ❑ The teacher told Justin that **EXPUNGING** the low grades from his record was not something she was willing to do.

FACILITATE
(fuh SIL uh tayt) *v.*
to make easier, to help bring about

Link: **CELL MATE**

"*You're lucky to have a **CELL MATE** who
FACILITATES a homey atmosphere.*"

- ❏ CDs **FACILITATE** learning a foreign language.
- ❏ In order to **FACILITATE** the sale of their home, George came down on the price.
- ❏ Jack's tools **FACILITATED** the repair of the sink.

FATHOM

(fa THUM) *v.*
to understand fully;
to penetrate the meaning of

Link: **FAT THUMB**

*"Doctors could never **FATHOM** the reason
for Larry's **FAT THUMB**."*

❑ Her friends thought they had **FATHOMED** the reason Estelle applied for entrance in an all-boys college: She never had any dates.

❑ The jury found it hard to **FATHOM** how the defendant could commit such a terrible crime.

❑ (In nautical terms, **FATHOM** is six feet of water depth.) We dropped anchor in four **FATHOMS** of water and made plans to stay for the night.

FAWN
(fawn) *v.*
to show affection

Link: **FAWN**

*"A **FAWN FAWNING** over his mother."*

- ❏ The head of the movie studio didn't see through the **FAWNING** of all his underlings, believing they truly thought he was a genius.

- ❏ Mr. Johnson was a professional at "sucking up" to everybody he thought could help him advance in his career, a professional **FAWNER** from the word go.

- ❏ The grandmother **FAWNED** over her grandchild, tickling him and making goo-goo sounds.

FEIGN

(fayn) *v.*
to give a false
appearance; to pretend

Link: **INSANE**

*"The prisoner FEIGNED INSANITY
as a defense to his crime."*

- Jeremy talked a good game but **FEIGNED** knowledge of space science he did not possess.

- Elizabeth **FEIGNED** illness in order to stay home from school on the day of her final exam.

- (Any **FEIGNED** action is a **FEINT**.) The boxer kept **FEINTING** with his left hand, waiting for an opening to hit a knockout punch with his right.

FESTER
(FES tur) *v.*
to generate pus; to become a source
of resentment or irritation

Link: **UNCLE FESTER**

*"**UNCLE FESTER** likes to pick his scabs
and watch them **FESTER**."*

❏ Diane's **FESTERING** resentments toward her
boss finally drove her to quit her job.

❏ Private Sholley's wounds had **FESTERED** for so
long it was nearly impossible for the surgeons to
save his leg.

❏ Coach Jones' resentments toward the complain-
ing players on the team **FESTERED** until he
finally told them to shut up or quit.

FETISH

(FET ish) *n.*
an object of unreasonable,
obsessive reverence or attention

Link: **BRITISH**

*"The **BRITISH**, they say, have an
absolute **FETISH** for tea.*

❑ Her psychologist said the reason Darlene had a
FETISH of washing her hands a dozen times a
day was because she had a guilt complex about
something in her past life, and she was trying to
wash the guilt away.

❑ Mary has a **FETISH** for chocolate, she hides a
box under her bed, in her desk at the office, and
in her purse.

FICKLE

(FIK ul) *adj.*
often changing for no reason;
not loyal or consistent

Link: **PICKLE**

*"Pregnant women are very **FICKLE**; one moment
they want ice cream, the next, **PICKLES**."*

❏ The summer weather is always very **FICKLE**,
each morning the sun shines, but when you are
ready to play golf, it starts to rain.

❏ Brad is a **FICKLE** eater; it's hard to say what he
likes to eat.

❏ Coach Adams' **FICKLENESS** was known by all
his players; he would say you were the best player
on the team, but would replace you the first time
you made a mistake.

FJORD
(fyord) *n.*
a long narrow inlet from the sea
between steep cliffs or hills

Link: **FORD**

"FORDS in a FJORD"

- ❑ Norway and New Zealand are two countries noted for having the most scenic **FJORDS** in the world.

- ❑ **FJORDS** are generally deep enough so that large cruise ships have more than enough water to navigate up their length.

- ❑ The Grand Canyon could be the grandest **FJORD** of all, if only it were on the coast with an inlet from the sea.

FLEECE

(flees) *v./n.*
to defraud, swindle; also the wool
of a sheep or similar animal

Link: **FLEEING**

"FLEEING with the FLEECE"

- ❑ It was spring on the Australian sheep farms, the time of year when the sheep are **FLEECED** for their wool.

- ❑ The housewives on our street were **FLEECED** by a con man selling bogus magazine subscriptions.

- ❑ Jim had larceny in his heart all his life and would sooner **FLEECE** a customer than make an honest deal.

FORTUITOUS
(for TWO uh tus) *n.*
good fortune occurring
by accident or chance

Link: **FORTUNE FOR THE TWO OF US**

**"A *FORTUITOUS FORTUNE*
FOR THE TWO OF US"**

❑ Arriving at the opera at the last moment, it was
FORTUITOUS there were seats available for the
two of us.

❑ "The most **FORTUITOUS** event of my entire life,"
said President Roosevelt, "was meeting my wife,
Eleanor."

❑ It was **FORTUITOUS** missing the ill-fated flight
because of the traffic jam on the way to the
airport.

FRAUGHT

(frawt) *n.*
teeming with; laden; full;
involving; accompanied by

Link: **CAUGHT**

*"Eric **CAUGHT** a boatload in
a lake **FRAUGHT** with fish."*

- ❏ The freighter was **FRAUGHT** with cargo.

- ❏ Although Mark Twain's books were **FRAUGHT** with humor, they nevertheless drove home good advice for their readers, young and old.

- ❏ Kathy was **FRAUGHT** with guilt about losing her temper with the children when she found out it wasn't their fault.

GAMIN

(GAM in) *n.*
a neglected boy left to
run about in the streets

Link: **JAMMIN'**

"A JAMMIN' GAMIN"

❑ In India, everywhere our tour bus stopped, there
would be a gang of **GAMINS** begging for money,
but if you dared give a rupee to one, a hundred
more would immediately appear.

❑ In the novel, *Oliver Twist*, we learn of the intoler-
able living conditions in English orphanages of
the nineteenth century and the life of the many
homeless, streetwise **GAMINS**.

❑ My dad always told me to stay in school and
study hard or I'd become a **GAMIN**.

GAZEBO

(guh ZEE boh) *n.*
an outdoor structure with
a roof and open sides

Link: **ZEBRA**

*"A **ZEBRA GAZEBO** on the Mari Mari
Plains of Kenya, East Africa"*

- ❏ A **GAZEBO** is most always found in a backyard or park.

- ❏ The **GAZEBO** in the mission courtyard was used for weddings in the summer. In the winter, goats would come and huddle together to stay warm and out of the rainy weather.

- ❏ On Sunday afternoons the family would gather together in the shade of our backyard **GAZEBO**.

GENERALIZE

(JEN ur ul ize) *v.*
general rather than specific;
to form a general conclusion

Link: **GENERAL'S EYES**

*"To say that all **GENERALS' EYES** are
the same is to **GENERALIZE**."*

- ❏ Wilma's problem was she always **GENERALIZED**. Everything was either always bad or always good, and she could never specifically say what she liked or disliked.

- ❏ Our teacher asked us to be specific when answering the test questions and avoid **GENERALIZING**.

- ❏ To say that all politicians are crooks and all lawyers are honest is to **GENERALIZE**.

GIDDY

(GID ee) *adj.*
a light-headed sensation;
dizzy; lightheartedly silly

Link: **CITY**

*"Farmer John gets a little **GIDDY**
every time he goes to the **CITY**."*

- ❏ After Sue won the beauty contest, she was absolutely **GIDDY** with joy.

- ❏ Jackie didn't faint, but she said the sun was so hot she felt **GIDDY**.

- ❏ Bill never had more than one beer; anything more made him **GIDDY**.

GIRD
(gird) *v.*
to encircle as with a belt;
to prepare as for action

Link: **HERD**

*"Curly **GIRDED** the **HERD**
with his trusty lasso."*

❏ Johnny's job each week of the soccer season
was to **GIRD** the field with a line of white chalk to
mark the boundaries of the playing field.

❏ Dad's bath robe is **GIRDED** with a terry cloth belt.

❏ **GIRDED** for action, the tanks moved forward into
battle formation.

Match the word with its definition.

___	1. forage	a.	teeming with; laden; full
___	2. forbear	b.	to encircle as with a belt
___	3. forsake	c.	lightheartedly silly
___	4. fortuitous	d.	good fortune occurring by accident
___	5. fraught	e.	a neglected boy left in the streets
___	6. gamin	f.	to abandon, to give up, to renounce
___	7. gazebo	g.	an outdoor structure
___	8. generalize	h.	to do without; to leave alone
___	9. giddy	i.	to search for food and provisions
___	10. gird	j.	general rather than specific

Fill in the blanks with the most appropriate word.
The word form may need changing.

1. After Sue won the beauty contest, she was absolutely _____ with joy.

2. After the campers fell asleep in their tents, the raccoons began _____ through the camp site for anything to eat.

3. Kathy was _____ with guilt about losing her temper with the children when she found out it wasn't their fault.

4. Our teacher asked us to be specific when answering the test questions and avoid _____ .

5. My dad always told me to stay in school and study hard or I'd become a _____ .

6. On Sunday afternoons the family would gather together in the shade of our backyard _____ .

7. It was _____ missing the ill-fated flight because of the traffic jam on the way to the airport.

8. Dad's bath robe is _____ with a terry cloth belt.

9. Sally said it was difficult to _____ smoking after doing it for twenty years.

10. The parents urged their daughter to _____ her career as a model and return to their home to become a school teacher.

GIRTH

(girth) *n.*
the distance around something;
to encircle; to secure with a band
that encircles the body of an animal

Link: **BIRTH**

*"Before giving **BIRTH**, ladies
are quite large in **GIRTH**."*

❑ Before crawling into a sewer pipe, it is first wise to measure its **GIRTH**.

❑ The **GIRTH** of the planet Earth is about twenty-five thousand miles.

❑ Jonathan placed the saddle on top of the horse and fastened the **GIRTH**.

GLOAT

(gloht) *v.*
to brag greatly

Link: **GOAT**

*"And I got this award for receiving so many awards," said the **GLOATING GOAT**.*

- ❑ For years she **GLOATED** over the marriage of her daughter to the most eligible bachelor in town.

- ❑ After winning the state championship last year, the football team **GLOATED** for a whole year until they lost the first game of the season.

- ❑ The mechanic said he didn't want to appear to **GLOAT**, but he did warn his customer last year he would have to fix it now or fix it later, and later would cost more.

GLUTTON
(GLUT en) *n.*
one who eats or consumes a great deal; having
capacity to receive or withstand something

Link: **GUT TON**

*"If you're a **GLUTTON**, your*
***GUT** could weigh a **TON**."*

❑ The neighbor's kids are such **GLUTTONS**,
whenever they come over they clean out the frig.

❑ Jack was a **GLUTTON** for punishment; no matter
how many times he was knocked down in the
fight, he kept getting up.

❑ A baseball freak, JoAnne **GLUTTONOUSLY**
reads every sports book on baseball she can get
her hands on.

GOSSAMER

(GOS uh mur) *n./adj.*
delicate floating cobwebs; a sheer gauzy
fabric; something delicate, light, flimsy

Link: **CUSTOMER**

*"The spider's **GOSSAMER** captured
many unhappy **CUSTOMERS**."*

❑ The bride wore a white silk wedding dress which
touched the floor as she proceeded up the aisle
to the altar. A **GOSSAMER** of fine Italian lace
gently touched her face.

❑ Between the audience and the actors on the
stage hung a thin **GOSSAMER** of fabric,
heightening the feeling that the actors were in a
dream-like setting.

❑ The **GOSSAMER** shawl she wore was not
enough to keep her warm in the frigid air.

GRANDILOQUENT
(gran DIL uh kwent) *adj.*
attempting to impress with big
words or grand gestures

Link: **GRAND ELEPHANT**

*"The **GRAND ELEPHANT** made a
GRANDILOQUENT speech."*

- ❏ It was another **GRANDILOQUENT** political affair; the candidates made the same old promises for lower taxes and more free services.

- ❏ They may be eloquent, but there is nothing grand about pompous **GRANDILOQUENT** speakers.

- ❏ The new teacher's **GRANDILOQUENCE** didn't fool the class one bit. She really knew very little about South American history.

GRANDIOSE
(GRAN dee ohs) *adj.*
grand and impressive, especially
flashy and showy

Link: **GRAND HOSE**

*"The **GRANDIOSE** Alaskan Pipeline resembles
nothing more than a **GRAND HOSE**."*

❑ Our coach had a **GRANDIOSE** plan to beat the
Dallas Cowboys, only he didn't count on the fact
that they had a **GRANDIOSE** plan of their own.

❑ In all respects it was a simple enough house,
unlike many others in that part of town. But the
one exception was the **GRANDIOSE** fireplace in
the family room, big enough to drive a truck
through.

❑ The director demanded a **GRANDIOSE** car chase
in his action movie.

GUILE

(gyle) *n.*
cunning, deceitfulness; artfulness

Link: **MILE**

Nobody could say Billy didn't use
__GUILE__ when running the __MILE__."

- ❑ Few people realized Bob's reputation as a shrewd businessman was due to his **GUILE**.

- ❑ The **GUILE** of the ticket scalper was shocking. He was selling tickets today for yesterday's tennis matches.

- ❑ (**BEGUILE** is different from **GUILE** in that it is deception in a charming way.) Lois **BEGUILED** her beau with fetching flirtations.

GUISE

(gize) *n.*
appearance, semblance

Link: **DISGUISE**

*"A master of DISGUISE, Sherlock
Holmes concealed his real GUISE."*

❏ Every night the undercover detective would enter
the toughest part of town in the **GUISE** of a
junkie, uncovering the identity of many drug
pushers.

❏ The undercover police car had the **GUISE** of a
typical family car.

❏ His awestruck **GUISE** looked as though he had
just witnessed a horrific accident.

HARANGUE
(huh RANG) *v.*
to lecture, berate; a long bombastic speech

Link: **MERINGUE**

*"The mayor's **HARANGUE** that women should stay home more was met with **MERINGUE** pies."*

- ❏ The sergeant **HARANGUED** his recruits for not keeping in step as the platoon practiced marching.

- ❏ Our neighbor is a farmer who goes to town once a week on Saturdays and **HARANGUES** everyone he meets on how bad the government treats farmers.

- ❏ A perpetual **HARANGUER**, Jeannie was a feminist who believed everyone who didn't believe as she did was an anti-feminist.

HARROWING
(HARE roe ing) *adj.*
extremely distressing; disturbing or frightening

Link: **HARE ROWING**

*"A **HARROWING** experience
for a **HARE ROWING**"*

- ❏ After the **HARROWING** experience when Eddie's main parachute didn't open, and his emergency chute saved him only at the last minute, he vowed never to jump again.

- ❏ (**HARRIED** is to be troubled or bothered while **HARROWING** is to be frightened to the extreme.) At first we were **HARRIED** by the gang members, called names and insulted, but later it became a **HARROWING** experience as they chased and threatened us with knives.

Match the word with its definition.

___ 1. girth	a. cunning, deceitfulness; artfulness
___ 2. gloat	b. one who eats a lot
___ 3. glutton	c. grand and impressive
___ 4. gossamer	d. extremely distressing or frightening
___ 5. grandiloquent	e. attempting to impress with big words
___ 6. grandiose	f. to brag greatly
___ 7. guile	g. to lecture, berate; a long speech
___ 8. guise	h. appearance, semblance
___ 9. harangue	i. something delicate, light, flimsy
___ 10. harrowing	j. the distance around something

Fill in the blanks with the most appropriate word. The word form may need changing.

1. The _____ shawl she wore was not enough to keep her warm in the frigid air.

2. The undercover police car had the _____ of a typical family car.

3. The _____ of the ticket scalper was shocking. He was selling tickets today for yesterday's tennis matches.

4. The neighbor's kids are such _____, whenever they come over they clean out the frig.

5. The _____ of the planet Earth is about twenty-five thousand miles.

6. After winning the state championship last year, the football team _____ for a whole year until they lost the first game of the season.

7. They may be eloquent, but there is nothing grand about pompous _____ speakers.

8. After the _____ experience when Eddie's main parachute didn't open, and his emergency chute saved him only at the last minute, he vowed never to jump again.

9. The sergeant _____ his recruits for not keeping in step as the platoon practiced marching.

10. The director demanded a _____ car chase in his action movie.

HERBICIDE

(HERB uh side) *n.*
a substance used to destroy
plants, especially weeds

Link: **SUICIDE**

*"When weeds commit **SUICIDE**,
they use a **HERBICIDE**."*

- ❏ Environmentalists have proven that **HERBICIDAL** runoffs from farmland pollute our rivers, streams, and oceans.

- ❏ Many farmers use **HERBICIDE** for controlling weeds on their farms.

- ❏ Ed completely destroyed his lawn after he mistook **HERBICIDE** for fertilizer.

HISTRIONIC

(his tree AHN ik) *adj.*
overly dramatic, theatrical

Link: **HISTORY**

*"Professor Bradley liked his **HISTORY**
on the **HISTRIONIC** side."*

- ❑ As soon as you would mention the word wrinkle, the middle-aged actress would fall into a state of **HISTRIONIC** tears.

- ❑ Everything Michael said was on the swaggering, **HISTRIONIC** side, as if he were the coolest guy on campus.

- ❑ The young actor's **HISTRIONIC** portrayal of his character was too much to bear.

HOARD

(hord) *v.*

to accumulate for future use; stockpile

Link: **STORED**

*"A squirrel **HOARDS** nuts, and **STORES**
them for the approaching winter."*

- ❑ Laura doesn't eat her Halloween candy, instead she likes to **HOARD** it and make it last all year.

- ❑ We told Ed there was no point in his **HOARDING** all the cake; he might as well share with us before it spoiled.

- ❑ The government announced during the national crisis that **HOARDERS** would be punished with jail sentences.

HOVEL

(HUV ul) *v.*
a small, miserable dwelling;
an open, low shed

Link: **SHOVEL**

*"The mice's **HOVEL** was an old, rusted **SHOVEL**."*

___

❑ In the famous play, *Tobacco Road*, the characters were poor tobacco farmers who live in **HOVELS**, shacks made of cardboard and discarded wooden boxes.

❑ Compared to the Summertons' palatial estate on Long Island, Jane said her apartment in the Bronx was a **HOVEL**.

❑ The poor live in **HOVELS** on the outskirts of town.

HUSBANDRY

(HUZ bun dree) *n.*
management of resources,
especially in agriculture

Link: **HUSBAND TREE**

*"To help in her **HUSBANDRY** chores, Aunt
Emma had her own **HUSBAND TREE**."*

- ❑ Bud's superb **HUSBANDRY** of his orange grove
  resulted in a larger than expected crop this year.

- ❑ (**HUSBANDRY** is the practice of conserving resources; to **HUSBAND** is to economize.) Experts
  say the world's oil resources will soon be
  exhausted, and we must soon begin to
  HUSBAND oil.

- ❑ Everyone in our squad **HUSBANDED** their share
  of water for the long trek back to the barracks.

IDIOSYNCRASY
(id ee oh SING kruh see) *n.*
a behavioral quirk; a person's idea about
behavior different from others

Link: **SINK CRAZY**

"Waldo's artistic **IDIOSYNCRASY**
is he's **SINK CRAZY**."

❑ Harriet had a way of smacking her lips every time you asked her a question, a seemingly harmless enough **IDIOSYNCRASY**, except that it drove you crazy after a while.

❑ Jimmy Chen's habit of eating soup as a last course is no **IDIOSYNCRASY**; most Chinese have soup last instead of first as is the American custom.

❑ Stan's **IDIOSYNCRASY** of constantly clicking his pen drove the whole class crazy.

IMPEDE

(im PEED) *v.*
to obstruct or interfere with; to delay

Link: **SPEED**

"The job of highway patrolmen is to
IMPEDE SPEEDING *motorists."*

❑ He was only my uncle, but he always told me no matter what, not to let anyone **IMPEDE** my ambition to go to medical school.

❑ (Something that **IMPEDES** is an **IMPEDIMENT**.) As a hopeful runner on the school track team, James Carver's biggest **IMPEDIMENT** to his speed was his short legs.

❑ The bad weather **IMPEDED** the climber's attempt to summit Mount Everest by nightfall.

INCITE
(in SIGHT) *v.*
to arouse to action

Link: **FIGHT**

*"The pitcher's bean ball INCITED
the batter to FIGHT."*

- ❑ The mob was **INCITED** to riot when the police arrived and began hitting people with their nightsticks.

- ❑ When Rodney decided that his case was hopeless, nothing the doctors could say would **INCITE** him to fight his illness.

- ❑ Waving a stick at Jerry's dog only **INCITES** him and increases the chance he will bite you.

INCONGRUOUS

(in KAHN grew us) *adj.*
not appropriate, unsuited to the
surroundings; not fitting in

Link: **IN CONGRESS**

*"The new Alaskan senator's presence IN
CONGRESS was INCONGRUOUS."*

- ❏ Ed appeared **INCONGRUOUS** wearing his
  tuxedo on an old-fashioned hayride.

- ❏ The **INCONGRUITY** with Joseph's chosen career
  was that he had a Ph.D. in chemistry, but
  preferred to work as a mullet fisherman.

- ❏ **INCONGRUOUSLY**, Dianne spent several days
  a week at the library, even though she professed
  that she didn't like to read.

INFAMY
(IN fah mee) *n.*
an evil reputation; extreme disgrace

Link: **FAMILY**

*"Blackbeard the Pirate's **FAMILY**
will live in **INFAMY**."*

- ❏ Western outlaws such as Jesse and Frank James have been made heroes in movies, but in reality they were **INFAMOUS** for their bad deeds.

- ❏ The **INFAMIES** of Germany's Adolf Hitler will live for eternity.

- ❏ The great white shark has been made **INFAMOUS** by the movie *Jaws*.

Match the word with its definition.

___ 1.	herbicide	a.	to obstruct or interfere with; to delay
___ 2.	histrionic	b.	a substance used to destroy weeds
___ 3.	hoard	c.	overly dramatic, theatrical
___ 4.	hovel	d.	a behavioral quirk
___ 5.	husbandry	e.	an evil reputation; extreme disgrace
___ 6.	idiosyncrasy	f.	to accumulate for future use; stockpile
___ 7.	impede	g.	management of resources
___ 8.	incite	h.	a small, miserable dwelling
___ 9.	incongruous	i.	to arouse to action
___ 10.	infamy	j.	not appropriate, unsuited to the surroundings; not fitting in

Fill in the blanks with the most appropriate word. The word form may need changing.

1. Stan's _____ of constantly clicking his pen drove the whole class crazy.

2. The poor live in _____ on the outskirts of town.

3. Waving a stick at Jerry's dog only _____ him and increases the chance he will bite you.

4. Laura doesn't eat her Halloween candy, instead she likes to _____ it and make it last all year.

5. The great white shark has been made _____ by the movie *Jaws*.

6. Ed appeared _____ wearing his tuxedo on an old-fashioned hayride.

7. The young actor's _____ portrayal of his character was too much to bear.

8. Bud's superb _____ of his orange grove resulted in a larger than expected crop this year.

9. Many farmers use _____ for controlling weeds on their farms.

10. The bad weather _____ the climber's attempt to summit Mount Everest by nightfall.

INSOUCIANT

(in SOO see unt) *adj.*
calm and carefree; lighthearted

Link: **SOUTH SEA ANT**

*"**SOUTH SEA ANTS** are the most
INSOUCIANT ants of all."*

- ❏ Children play **INSOUCIANTLY**, as if they did not have a care in the world.

- ❏ Jake's **INSOUCIANT** behavior was inappropriate at his grandfather's funeral. It lacked respect for his memory.

- ❏ Bob's **INSOUCIANT** demeanor in the locker room before the big game meant he was extremely confident that we would win.

INTERVENE

(in tur VEEN) *v.*
to come between; to mediate,
to occur between times

Link: **BETWEEN**

*"Referees INTERVENE
BETWEEN player disputes."*

❑ Harold and his twin brother might have argued
all day if their father hadn't **INTERVENED** and
said that if they couldn't decide who would ride
in the front seat, they would both ride in the
back.

❑ Our teenage daughter doesn't like it when her
mother and I **INTERVENE** in her social life.

❑ So much had happened to the family in the
INTERVENING years since Brett had gone off
to college.

INVEIGLE
(in VAY gul) *v.*
to tempt or persuade
by using deception or flattery

Link: **BAGEL**

*"The animal trainer **INVEIGLED** the lion to
perform by tempting him with a **BAGEL**."*

❑ My brother, Ryan, **INVEIGLED** me into doing his
chemistry homework by promising to take my
turn washing dishes for the next week.

❑ New York City street vendors **INVEIGLE** people
into purchasing counterfeit Rolex watches for
many times what they are worth.

❑ Laura **INVEIGLED** her history teacher into
allowing her to retake the mid-term exam she
missed because she overslept.

IRASCIBLE
(ih RAS uh bul) *adj.*
easily angered, irritable

Link: **WRESTLE BULLS**

*"When he became **IRASCIBLE**, the Masked Marvel would **WRESTLE BULLS**."*

- ❑ Normally, Rose was a pleasant wife and mother but if a member of her family prevented her from watching her favorite "soaps," she could become quite **IRASCIBLE**.

- ❑ Uncle Tim was a real grouch, even on his birthday he would find a way to become as **IRASCIBLE** as a spoiled child.

- ❑ The school principal became so **IRASCIBLE** even his teachers avoided speaking to him.

JOUST
(joust) *v./n.*
to engage in combat or competition;
any combat suggestive of a joust

Link: **MOUSE**

*"A **JOUSTING MOUSE** in King Arthur's time"*

❑ Running and enjoying the competition, Bill and Harry **JOUSTED** each other playfully.

❑ It was a **JOUST** to the death between Sir Lancelot and the Black Knight.

❑ Her toes all bruised, Elizabeth declared it wasn't a dance, but a **JOUSTING** match.

SAT WORD POWER   **217**

KARMA
(KAHR muh) *n.*
fate, destiny; the force generated
by a person's good or bad actions

Link: **HARM-A**

*"No **HARM-A** will come if you have good **KARMA**."*

- ❑ All his life he possessed a protective **KARMA** that kept him out of harm's way.

- ❑ Louise often told her friends it was her **KARMA** to die young and beautiful.

- ❑ Genghis Khan likely got a lot of bad **KARMA** for all the death and destruction he caused.

LACONIC
(luh KAHN ik) *adj.*
brief, using few words

Link: **TONIC**

*"Grandma was **LACONIC** when it
came time for Grandpa's **TONIC**."*

- ❏ Benjamin's **LACONIC** speech habits gave him a reputation for thoughtfulness and intelligence.

- ❏ The president's **LACONIC** speech only lasted ten minutes, when it usually takes an hour.

- ❏ The fictional heroes of the old west were usually cowboys who spoke **LACONICALLY**, when at all.

LAMENT

(luh MENT) *v.*
to express sorrow
or regret; to mourn

Link: **CEMENT**

*"We **LAMENT** that Joe
got buried in **CEMENT**."*

- ☐ There must have been thousands of people at the funeral to **LAMENT** the death of Princess Diane.

- ☐ The nation **LAMENTS** the passing of the President while at the same time celebrating his achievements while in office.

- ☐ It is **LAMENTABLE** that Roscoe quit college in his sophomore year; his professors considered him the brightest engineering student in his class.

LANGUISH
(LANG gwish) *v.*
to become weak or feeble;
sag with loss of strength

Link: **LAND FISH**

*"A **FISH** on **LAND** will quickly **LANGUISH**."*

❑ An outdoorsman all his life, Mr. Franklin quickly **LANGUISHED** in his job as a night watchman.

❑ It was so hot in the theater, Charlotte soon began to **LANGUISH**.

❑ Running in his first marathon, Kevin began to **LANGUISH** with only a mile to go.

LASSITUDE
(LAS uh tood) *n.*
a condition of weariness; fatigue

Link: **LAZY DUDE**

*"A **LAZY DUDE** with **LASSITUDE**"*

- After eating three servings of Thanksgiving dinner, George succumbed to a feeling of **LASSITUDE** and fell asleep on the couch.

- The troops overcame their **LASSITUDE** and marched another five miles through knee-deep of snow.

- Weakened by a full day of traveling, **LASSITUDE** finally overcame the weary travelers.

Match the word with its definition.

__	1. insouciant	a. easily angered, irritable
__	2. intervene	b. a condition of weariness
__	3. inveigle	c. brief, using few words
__	4. irascible	d. to become weak or feeble
__	5. joust	e. fate, destiny
__	6. karma	f. to tempt by using deception
__	7. laconic	g. to express sorrow or regret; to mourn
__	8. lament	h. to engage in combat or competition
__	9. languish	i. calm and carefree; lighthearted
__	10. lassitude	j. to come between; to mediate, to occur between times

Fill in the blanks with the most appropriate word.
The word form may need changing.

1. It was a _____ to the death between Sir Lancelot and the Black Knight.

2. The school principal became so _____ even his teachers avoided speaking to him.

3. There must have been thousands of people at the funeral to _____ the death of Princess Diane.

4. Our teenage daughter doesn't like it when her mother and I _____ in her social life.

5. The president's _____ speech only lasted ten minutes, when it usually takes an hour.

6. Bob's _____ demeanor in the locker room before the big game meant he was extremely confidant that we would win.

7. Laura _____ her history teacher into allowing her to retake the mid-term exam she missed because she overslept.

8. Running in his first marathon, Kevin began to _____ with only a mile to go.

9. Weakened by a full day of traveling, _____ finally overcame the weary travelers.

10. Louise often told her friends it was her _____ to die young and beautiful.

LAUDABLE
(LAWD uh bul) *adj.*
worthy or deserving of praise

Link: **APPLAUDABLE**

"A **LAUDABLE** performance
that was **APPLAUDABLE**"

❑ Hector's teacher told him she thought it most
LAUDABLE that he wanted to become a doctor,
but an F in biology was not going to help him
achieve his goal.

❑ David's **LAUDABLE** performance on the football
field was a big part of the reason his team won
the state championship.

❑ The president's **LAUDABLE** speech ended with
a standing ovation.

LAX

(lax) *adj.*
careless, negligent; not tense, slack

Link: **TAX**

*"This is what happens when you're
LAX in paying your **TAX**."*

- ❑ The bank robbers planned to rob the bank when security was **LAX**.

- ❑ Most bachelors are **LAX** in their housekeeping, but Mike and Bob set a record for **LAXITY**, as they only washed eating utensils when they were ready to eat.

- ❑ When they arrived at the dock, they found the ropes were **LAX**, and their boat was bumping against the dock.

LEGACY

(LEG uh see) *n.*
something handed down from one who has
gone before or from the past; a bequest

Link: **LEG I SEE**

*"The **LEG I SEE** is my entire **LEGACY** from
Great-Grandfather Paul the Pirate."*

- ❑ The **LEGACY** of the copper mining industry is
  the creation of mountains of waste where
  beautiful, unspoiled forests once stood.

- ❑ The fictional **LEGACIES** of the Old West in the
  late 1800s was of cowboys riding from town to
  town shooting at each other.

- ❑ The Johnson family's ancestral **LEGACY** was to
  have blonde hair and green eyes.

LESION

(LEE zhun) *n.*
wound, injury; especially one
created by a disease

Link: **LEGION**

*"Soldiers of the French Foreign **LEGION**
suffering from their **LESIONS**"*

- ❏ The nurses told Crystal to keep the bandage on
  her knee until the **LESION** healed, otherwise the
  open sore would be prone to infection by airborne
  bacteria.

- ❏ When a person has a **LESION**, even a small one
  that will not heal, it is time to see a doctor.

- ❏ Ebola is an infectious disease characterized by
  open **LESIONS** of the skin.

LETHARGY
(LETH ur gee) *n.*
laziness, tiredness; languor

Link: **LEOPARD'S TEA**

*"**LETHARGIC LEOPARDS** having **TEA**"*

- ❑ There is nothing **LETHARGIC** about a cheetah chasing prey, as cheetahs are the fastest animals on earth.

- ❑ **LETHARGY** overcame everyone after eating a huge Thanksgiving dinner.

- ❑ His doctor told Jim he was in good health. His **LETHARGY** at work and at home was probably due to his being overweight, eating too much, and exercising too little.

LEXICON

(LEX a kon) *n.*
a dictionary; vocabulary terms used in or
of a particular profession, subject, or style

Link: **MEXICAN**

*"A **MEXICAN** reading his **LEXICON**"*

❑ The **LEXICON** used by air traffic controllers is
incomprehensible to non-pilots: "down wind to
twenty seven, hold three twenty at two thousand,
traffic at eleven o'clock, two miles."

❑ Sailors have a nautical **LEXICON**; "port means
left, starboard means right, bow means front, and
stern means rear."

❑ The confident general told his troops that defeat
was a term that did not exist in his **LEXICON**.

Link: **BREW**

*"In **LIEU** of a **BREW**, Billy
The Kid had an orange soda."*

- ❑ In **LIEU** of entering the university in September, Roger decided to work and save some money and start in January.

- ❑ Not wanting to lose her amateur standing after winning the U.S. Open singles title, Faye accepted the silver trophy in **LIEU** of the $545,000 first prize check.

- ❑ In **LIEU** of driving our own car to the restaurant, we decided to take a taxi.

LOITER

(LOY ter) *v.*
to remain in an area without
any specific reason; to lag behind

Link: **LAWYER**

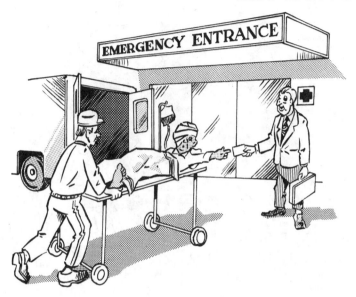

*"Ambulance-chasing **LAWYERS LOITER**
outside hospitals waiting for customers."*

- ❑ A sign outside the players' entrance to the stadium said, "No **LOITERING**," but autograph hounds **LOITERED** there before and after games anyway.

- ❑ The supporting actor was on stage during most of the play, but he was so ineffective it was almost as if he were a **LOITERER**.

- ❑ It is against the rules to **LOITER** on school grounds on the weekends.

MAIM

(maim) *v.*
to disable or disfigure, to cripple

Link: **BLAME**

*"Roger **MAIMED** the bear's
ear and **BLAMED** Walter."*

- ❏ Joshua was a private in the US Army and saw action in the invasion of France where on the sixteenth day after the landing, he was **MAIMED** when he stepped on a land mine and lost his leg.

- ❏ Every year people are **MAIMED** in automobile accidents by drunk drivers, the major cause of highway accidents.

- ❏ The **MAIMED** deer scurried into the woods after being wounded by the hunter's arrow.

MARAUDER
(muh RAWD er) *n.*
a raider, intruder

Link: **MA RAIDER**

"The fiercest MARAUDERS are MA RAIDERS."

- ❏ Among the legendary pirate **MARAUDERS** of the eighteenth century were Captain Kidd, Calico Jack Rackam, Charles Vane, Blackbeard, and Sir Henry Morgan.

- ❏ Christine referred to her husband, Christopher, as a kitchen **MARAUDER** for his midnight raids on the ice box.

- ❏ During the Civil War, **MARAUDING** bands of Confederate guerrillas raided Union supply lines in the Midwest.

Match the word with its definition.

___ 1. laudable	a.	something handed down
___ 2. lax	b.	a wound, injury
___ 3. legacy	c.	worthy or deserving of praise
___ 4. lesion	d.	careless, negligent; not tense, slack
___ 5. lethargy	e.	instead of; in place of
___ 6. lexicon	f.	a raider, intruder
___ 7. lieu	g.	a dictionary
___ 8. loiter	h.	to disable or disfigure, to cripple
___ 9. maim	i.	laziness, tiredness; languor
___ 10. marauder	j.	to remain in an area without any specific reason; to lag behind

Fill in the blanks with the most appropriate word.
The word form may need changing.

1. Among the legendary pirate _____ of the eighteenth century were Captain Kidd, Calico Jack Rackam, Charles Vane, Blackbeard, and Sir Henry Morgan.

2. It is against the rules to _____ on school grounds on the weekends.

3. Sailors have a nautical _____; "port means left, starboard means right, bow means front, and stern means rear."

4. The _____ of the copper mining industry is the creation of mountains of waste where beautiful, unspoiled forests once stood.

5. The _____ deer scurried into the woods after being wounded by the hunter's arrow.

6. The bank robbers planned to rob the bank when security was _____.

7. The president's _____ speech ended with a standing ovation.

8. In _____ of driving our own car to the restaurant, we decided to take a taxi.

9. Ebola is an infectious disease characterized by open _____ of the skin.

10. _____ overcame everyone after eating a huge Thanksgiving dinner.

MARSHAL

(MAHR shul) *v./n.*
to assemble together for the purpose of doing
something; also an officer in the police or military

Link: **MARSHAL**

*"The **MARSHAL MARSHALED** a
posse to capture the Waco Kid."*

- ❑ **MARSHALING** their forces, the British defeated Rommel at El Alamein.

- ❑ The Republicans **MARSHALED** their voters to firmly defeat the Democrats in the Congressional elections of 1994.

- ❑ The defense team **MARSHALED** its arguments before presenting them to the jury.

MARTYR

(MAHR tur) *n.*
someone willing to sacrifice and even
give his/her life for a cause; also one
who pretends suffering to gain sympathy

Link: **HARDER**

*"It's **HARDER** to be a **MARTYR**."*

- ❑ She was a professional **MARTYR**, all-suffering for her children, or so she would tell them ten times a day.

- ❑ Joan of Arc was undoubtedly the most famous **MARTYR** in modern history, burned at the stake because she refused to go against her beliefs.

- ❑ Jack was a **MARTYR** to his job; he worked seven days a week and rarely took a day off.

Link: **MAST ATE**

"LITTLE HENRY'S MASTICATING!!"

"POOR BABY'S TEETHING!"

*"Henry **ATE** the **MAST** when he started to **MASTICATE**."*

❑ The doctor explained that a person's digestion is aided when they **MASTICATE** their food thoroughly.

❑ The Kiwi bird **MASTICATES** food before giving it to its young.

❑ The judge requested a recess to **MASTICATE** the facts presented by both the prosecution and the defense.

MELANCHOLY
(MEL un kahl ee) *n.*
depression of spirits; gloomy; weary

Link: **MELON**

*"Farmer Brown was beset with
MELANCHOLY when he saw what the
worms had done to his MELON patch."*

- ❑ Sitting in her living room and thinking of her late husband brought a touch of **MELANCHOLY** to Aunt Mildred's remembrances of Uncle John.

- ❑ The best word to describe Jim is **MELANCHOLY**; no matter the situation, he always walks around looking like he had lost his best friends.

- ❑ It was a **MELANCHOLY** day, gloomy and dark.

MENAGERIE
(muh NAJ uh ree) *n.*
a collection of live wild animals on exhibit

Link: **LINGERIE**

"A MENAGERIE of LINGERIE"

❑ Busch Gardens has a wonderful **MENAGERIE** of lions, tigers, elephants, and other wild animals roaming free and on display in a park-like setting.

❑ To have a house pet is one thing, but Susan keeps so many parrots and cats in her house, it is a virtual **MENAGERIE**.

❑ With twelve children in the family, the Jacksons referred to their offspring as their **MENAGERIE**.

MIGRATORY
(MY gruh tor ee) *adj.*
roving, wandering, nomadic

Link: **MY STORY**

*"**MY STORY** is one of many
MIGRATORY movements."*

- ❑ Wild geese **MIGRATE** to Canada in the summers and Mexico in the winters.

- ❑ Most American Indian tribes in the Old West were **MIGRATORY** and followed the movements of the buffalo.

- ❑ Fruit pickers are **MIGRATORY** workers who move from place to place at harvesting time.

MILIEU
(meel YOO) *n.*
environment or surroundings

Link: **MILDEW**

*"The boys' locker room showers
were a **MILIEU** of **MILDEW**."*

- ❏ After a long sea journey, a sailor on land for the first few days feels out of his **MILIEU**.

- ❏ The proper **MILIEU** for raising a family is a home setting with loving parents who understand child rearing; something every parent must work at and not take for granted.

- ❏ The New York Stock Exchange is a **MILIEU** of frenzied activity during trading hours.

MIRAGE
(muh RAJ) *n.*
unreal reflection; an optical illusion

Link: **GARAGE**

*"The **GARAGE** they thought they saw crossing the desert was only a **MIRAGE**."*

- ❏ Her beauty was mostly a **MIRAGE** created by the art of cosmetics.

- ❏ Desert caravans often see **MIRAGES** on days when heat waves are reflected off the burning sands.

- ❏ The **MIRAGE** of the lake was a welcome sight to the parched desert traveler until he bent down to take a drink and got a mouthful of sand.

MISANTHROPY
(mis AN thruh pee) *n.*
someone who hates mankind

Link: **MISS ANTHROPY**

"*MISS ANTHROPY* was
a *MISANTHROPIC* person."

❏ A more **MISANTHROPIC** person you never did
see. He hates everyone.

❏ Adolph Hitler is known for his **MISANTHROPY**.

❏ Some people live their entire lives never realizing
they have a **MISANTHROPIC** attitude about the
world, because first and foremost they have
never liked themselves.

MISNOMER
(mis NOH mur) *n.*
an incorrect or inappropriate name

Link: **MISS HOMER**

*"What a **MISNOMER**, our little **MISS HOMER** struck out five times in a row."*

- ❏ A nickname like "Speedy" is a **MISNOMER** when directed toward one who is slow at what they do.

- ❏ We usually have dinner at this very small Italian restaurant called The Spaghetti Factory, obviously a **MISNOMER** of major proportions.

- ❏ It was no **MISNOMER** when they called Harry Houdini, "The Great Houdini," as he was the greatest escape artist of his time.

VOCABULARY CARTOONS Review #21

Match the word with its definition.

___ 1. marshal	a. someone willing to sacrifice
___ 2. martyr	b. to chew
___ 3. masticate	c. to assemble together
___ 4. melancholy	d. unreal reflection; an optical illusion
___ 5. menagerie	e. an incorrect or inappropriate name
___ 6. migratory	f. roving, wandering, nomadic
___ 7. milieu	g. someone who hates mankind
___ 8. mirage	h. environment or surroundings
___ 9. misanthropy	i. depression of spirits; gloomy; weary
___ 10. misnomer	j. a collection of live wild animals

Fill in the blanks with the most appropriate word.
The word form may need changing.

1. Desert caravans often see _____ on days when heat waves are reflected off the burning sands.

2. _____ their forces, the British defeated Rommel at El Alamein.

3. The New York Stock Exchange is a _____ of frenzied activity during trading hours.

4. Busch Gardens has a wonderful _____ of lions, tigers, elephants, and other wild animals roaming free and on display in a park-like setting.

5. A nickname like "Speedy" is a _____ when directed toward one who is slow at what they do.

6. The doctor explained that a person's digestion is aided when they _____ their food thoroughly.

7. Fruit pickers are _____ workers who move from place to place at harvesting time.

8. Joan of Arc was undoubtedly the most famous _____ in modern history, burned at the stake because she refused to go against her beliefs.

9. Adolph Hitler is known for his _____.

10. It was a _____ day, gloomy and dark.

245

MODE

(mowd) *n.*
a way or method of doing
something; type, manner, fashion

Link: **TOAD**

*"**TOADS** have a special
MODE for catching dinner."*

- ❑ Four-wheel drive vehicles have gears to go from two to four wheel drive **MODE**.

- ❑ Once he became a lawyer, Hal put aside his jeans and dressed in the **MODE** of his contemporaries, conservative dark suits, white shirts, and ties.

- ❑ Our vacation was in a laid-back **MODE**, sleeping-in late and then catching rays on the beach.

MORES

(MAWR ayz) *n.*
customary cultural standards;
moral attitudes, manners, habits

Link: **MORE As**

*"Our educational **MORES** have it that the **MORE As**
a student makes, the better their education."*

❑ According to Chinese **MORES**, it is considered
polite for dinner guests to belch at the table as a
gesture of appreciation and enjoyment.

❑ It is said that a certain actress of her
acquaintance has dubious morals and disregards
the accepted **MORES** for married women.

❑ The problem with some community **MORES** is
that the older generation clings to outdated moral
attitudes no longer appropriate for the times.

MUSE

(myooz) *v.*
to ponder; meditate; think about at length

Link: **FUSE**

*"Don't **MUSE** once the **FUSE** is lit."*

- ❑ Rick was such a good auto mechanic he never **MUSED** over what the problem might be; he knew immediately and went right to work fixing it.

- ❑ Chess is a **MUSING** game of skill whereupon each player **MUSES** over all the possible moves before deciding which piece to move.

- ❑ Though the odds of winning the lottery are very low, it is fun to **MUSE** about what you would do if you actually won.

MUSTER
(MUS tur) *v./n.*
to collect or gather; the act of
inspection or critical examination

Link: **MUSTARD**

*"Each morning the **MUSTARD** troops
are **MUSTERED** for roll call."*

- ❏ In 1836 the Texans at the Alamo **MUSTERED** all
  the troops available to defend against the
  invading Mexican Army.

- ❏ The restaurant owner inspected the kitchen and
  said the eating utensils did not pass **MUSTER**,
  and for the dish washer to wash them all over
  again.

- ❏ Dan **MUSTERED** all his strength to lift the weight
  over his head.

MYRIAD
(MIR ee ud) *n.*
an extremely large number

Link: **MIRROR ADD**

*"Many **MIRRORS ADD** a
MYRIAD of reflections."*

- ❑ After graduating from Harvard with a master's degree in business, Paul had a **MYRIAD** of career opportunities ahead of him.

- ❑ On a clear night in Alaska the sky is filled with a **MYRIAD** of stars.

- ❑ Jane said she had a **MYRIAD** of things to do to get ready for the party.

NEPOTISM

(NEP uh tiz um) *n.*
favors shown by those in high
positions to relatives and friends

Link: **NEPHEWISM**

*"Mr. Roberts, the CEO of the company, shows a
little **NEPOTISM** toward his **NEPHEW**."*

❑ Totally inept, Howard was a real estate agent for
the company only because his uncle, the
president, was not above a little **NEPOTISM**.

❑ The boss told his son that he didn't believe in
NEPOTISM and that he would have to work just
as hard as everyone else to get a promotion.

❑ The players knew it was **NEPOTISM** when the
coach named his son starting quarterback even
though he was the worst player on the team.

NOISOME
(NOY sum) *adj.*
stinking; offensive; disgusting

Link: **ANNOY SOME**

*"Inconsiderate, **NOISOME** smokers
are likely to **ANNOY SOME**."*

- ☐ Tobacco smoke is now considered so **NOISOME** in the majority of public places that smoking has become off limits.

- ☐ The comedian's act was absolutely **NOISOME**; all of his jokes depended entirely on four-lettered vulgarities.

- ☐ When I opened the garbage can, the odor was so **NOISOME** I thought I might suffocate before I could get the lid back on.

NOXIOUS

(NAWKS shus) *adj.*
physically or mentally destructive,
or harmful to human beings

Link: **KNOCKS US**

*"Her cheap perfume was so **NOXIOUS**,
it almost **KNOCKED US** out."*

❑ The **NOXIOUS** pollutants discharged into the bay by the paper mill killed all the marine life.

❑ The **NOXIOUS** waste produced by nuclear power plants is stored in special containers.

❑ (**OBNOXIOUS** is to be exposed to something **NOXIOUS**.) Jenny's flirtatious behavior with her best friend's husband was **OBNOXIOUS**.

OBLIQUE
(oh BLEEK) *adj.*
at an angle neither perpendicular
or parallel; indirect or evasive;
not straightforward

Link: **FREAK**

*"Folks are not **FREAKS** just
because they walk **OBLIQUELY**."*

- ❑ The architect's design featured **OBLIQUE** angles which made the home unique to the neighborhood.

- ❑ An **OBLIQUE** triangle has no right angles.

- ❑ The politician's **OBLIQUE** answers to the press's questions raised many questions about his integrity.

OBTUSE
(ob TOOS) *adj.*
lacking intelligence, difficult to comprehend; an angle greater than 90 degrees and less than 180 degrees

Link: **NOOSE**

*"Don't be **OBTUSE**; the horse-thief gets the **NOOSE**, not the horse."*

❑ The **OBTUSE** boy failed every class.

❑ Our attorney said that the contract was so **OBTUSELY** written that she had to rewrite the whole thing.

❑ **OBTUSE** and **OBLIQUE** angles are neither parallel or perpendicular, but **OBLIQUE** angles can be less than 90 degrees.

Match the word with its definition.

___ 1. mode	a.	to collect or gather
___ 2. mores	b.	harmful to human beings
___ 3. muse	c.	customary cultural standards
___ 4. muster	d.	a way or method of doing something
___ 5. myriad	e.	to ponder; to think about at length
___ 6. nepotism	f.	favors given to relatives and friends
___ 7. noisome	g.	an extremely large number
___ 8. noxious	h.	indirect or evasive
___ 9. oblique	i.	lacking intelligence
___ 10. obtuse	j.	stinking; offensive; disgusting

Fill in the blanks with the most appropriate word. The word form may need changing.

1. Dan _____ all his strength to lift the weight over his head.

2. The politician's _____ answers to the press's questions raised many questions about his integrity.

3. The players knew it was _____ when the coach named his son starting quarterback even though he was the worst player on the team.

4. Though the odds of winning the lottery are very low, it is fun to _____ about what you would do if you actually won.

5. After graduating from Harvard with a master's degree in business, Paul had a _____ of career opportunities ahead of him.

6. The _____ boy failed every class.

7. Once he became a lawyer, Hal put aside his jeans and dressed in the _____ of his contemporaries, conservative dark suits, white shirts, and ties.

8. The _____ pollutants discharged into the bay by the paper mill killed all the marine life.

9. According to Chinese _____ , it is considered polite for dinner guests to belch at the table as a gesture of appreciation and enjoyment.

10. The comedian's act was absolutely _____ ; all of his jokes depended entirely on four-lettered vulgarities.

OPPORTUNE
(ah pur TYOON) *adj.*
occurring or coming at a good time

Link: **OPERA TUNE**

*"This is not an OPPORTUNE
time for an OPERA TUNE."*

❑ An **OPPORTUNIST** at heart, Ed **OPPORTUNELY** dropped by Janet's house just as dinner was being served.

❑ During the family reunion, Christopher felt it the **OPPORTUNE** moment for announcing his job promotion.

❑ Mrs. Childs, our teacher, said the weekend before our final exam was an **OPPORTUNE** time for last minute studying.

OPTIMUM

(OP tuh mum) *n./adj.*
the most advantageous; the best
condition, degree, or amount

Link: **OCTOPUS MOM**

*"An **OCTOPUS MOM** has the
OPTIMUM ability to feed her young."*

- ❑ As the conditions were **OPTIMUM**, with no wind at the track, the U.S. Olympic team had hopes of breaking the world record in the 440 yard relay.

- ❑ In order to successfully jump 15 school buses, only motorcycle daredevil Evel Knievel knew what the **OPTIMUM** speed was that he needed to reach.

- ❑ With Rudy unemployed, his wife in the hospital, and the three children sick with the flu, this was hardly an **OPTIMUM** situation for the family.

ORTHODOX

(OR thuh dahks) *adj.*
conventional, doing it by the book,
sticking to established principles

Link: **THROW ROCKS**

"In the times of the Roman Empire, it was
***ORTHODOX* to *THROW ROCKS*.**"

- An **ORTHODOX** religion is one that holds fast to historical views that have not changed.

- The doctor's treatment for Judith's broken finger was **ORTHODOX**. He X-rayed the finger, set it in a splint, and told her to come back in a week.

- The **ORTHODOX** view of the earth is that it is round. The views of those who still believe the world is flat, as many did in the thirteenth century, is **UNORTHODOX**.

OSTRACIZE
(AHS truh size) *v.*
to exclude from a group; to shun

Link: **OSTRICH**

*"Ozzie the **OSTRICH** wondered why he was being **OSTRACIZED** from the group."*

❑ Andre felt **OSTRACIZED** by the members of the club, but the truth was they couldn't understand his accent.

❑ The popular girls at school **OSTRACIZED** anyone from their group that didn't wear designer clothes.

❑ After gaining a reputation as a cheap-shot player with the Pittsburgh Steelers, he joined the Dallas Cowboys only to find he was **OSTRACIZED** by the Dallas players as well.

Link: **HOUSE**

*"The landlord **OUSTED** the tenant from the
HOUSE when he didn't pay his rent."*

❑ Brett was caught with an alcoholic beverage and
was immediately **OUSTED** from the school
dance.

❑ The spectators in his part of the stands wanted to
have Roger **OUSTED** for making too much noise
during the tennis match.

❑ Later, after Roger's **OUSTER** by the ushers, he
complained to the management that he should
be allowed to cheer anytime he wanted.

PARADOX

(PAIR uh dahks) *n.*
a situation in which something
seems both true and false

Link: **BEARS OR DUCKS**

*"The 'are we **BEARS** or **DUCKS**' **PARADOX**"*

- ❑ A concrete boat is a great example of a **PARADOX**.

- ❑ John said he was an agnostic, but the **PARADOX** was he attended church every Sunday.

- ❑ Herbert's hatred of walking was **PARADOXICAL**, once you understood he worked as a mailman.

PARANOIA
(par uh NOY uh) *n.*
a mental illness of unreasonable anxiety,
especially believing someone is out to get
you, or that you are an important person

Link: **DESTROY 'YA**

*"**PARANOIA** will **DESTROY** 'YA."*

- ❏ Julie's **PARANOIA** was so advanced she thought everyone who came to her door was an assassin who had come to kill her.

- ❏ (A person suffering from **PARANOIA** is said to be **PARANOID**.) Joshua was absolutely **PARANOID** about walking under a ladder.

- ❏ When Ramon told his wife she was **PARANOID** about her hair, he meant she was very sensitive to criticism.

PARRY

(PAIR ee) *v.*
to ward off a blow; to turn aside;
to avoid skillfully, to evade

Link: **PEAR**

*"The **PEARS PARRIED** each
other's fencing movements."*

❑ The boxers **PARRIED** blows as each waited for
an opening to strike a knockout punch.

❑ **PARRYING** with respective verbal arguments,
the politicians blamed each other for the increase
in statewide crime.

❑ The knights charged Robin Hood's men, who
PARRIED their lances with limbs from the trees
in Sherwood Forest.

PARTITION

(par TISH un) *n.*
the division of something into parts;
an interior structure dividing a larger area

Link: **MAGICIAN**

*"The **MAGICIAN** creates a **PARTITION**"*

- ❑ Korea was originally one country before being **PARTITIONED** into North and South.

- ❑ The beds in the emergency room were **PARTITIONED** with portable screens for the patient's privacy.

- ❑ In most tennis clubs there are fence **PARTITIONS** separating the courts from each other.

PENITENT

(PEN uh tunt) *n./adj.*
one who feels sorrow and remorse for
past misdeeds; feeling sorrow or humble

Link: **PENITENTIARY**

*"Bubba was **PENITENT** for the crimes that
landed him in the **PENITENTIARY**."*

- ☐ Clark became **PENITENT** when he learned his careless driving had put two people in the hospital.

- ☐ The **PENITENT** young boys apologized for breaking the neighbor's window.

- ☐ Jennifer felt **PENITENT** that she had caused her mother so much sorrow.

Match the word with its definition.

___ 1. opportune   a. to exclude from a group; to shun
___ 2. optimum   b. sticking to established principles
___ 3. orthodox   c. the best condition or amount
___ 4. ostracize   d. an opposite truth
___ 5. oust   e. to ward off a blow; to turn aside
___ 6. paradox   f. mental illness of unreasonable anxiety
___ 7. paranoia   g. to eject; to force out; to banish
___ 8. parry   h. occurring or coming at a good time
___ 9. partition   i. feeling sorrow or humble
___ 10. penitent   j. the division of something into parts

Fill in the blanks with the most appropriate word.
The word form may need changing.

1. The popular girls at school _____ anyone from their group that didn't wear designer clothes.

2. The boxers _____ blows as each waited for an opening to strike a knockout punch.

3. The beds in the emergency room were _____ with portable screens for the patient's privacy.

4. Brett was caught with an alcoholic beverage and was immediately _____ from the school dance.

5. The _____ young boys apologized for breaking the neighbor's window.

6. In order to successfully jump 15 school buses, only motorcycle daredevil Evel Knievel knew what the _____ speed was that he needed to reach.

7. An _____ religion is one that holds fast to historical views that have not changed.

8. Julie's _____ was so advanced she thought everyone who came to her door was an assassin who had come to kill her.

9. Mrs. Childs, our teacher, said the weekend before our final exam was an _____ time for last minute studying.

10. John said he was an agnostic, but the _____ was he attended church every Sunday.

PERIPHERY

(puh RIF uh ree) *n.*
the outermost part within a
boundary, the outside edge

Link: **REFEREE**

*"**REFEREES** would be wise to stay outside
the **PERIPHERY** of a boxer's reach."*

- ❏ On the **PERIPHERY** of any argument, Jasmine
  will listen but rarely ever speak.

- ❏ Colonel Mason posted guards at the
  PERIPHERY of the camp for night security.

- ❏ What you see out of the corner of your eyes is
  your **PERIPHERAL** vision (looking straight ahead
  but seeing to the side).

PERMEATE

(PUR mee ayt) *v.*
to flow or spread through; penetrate

Link: **WORM HE ATE**

IT CLEARS THE SINUSES!

*"The **WORMS HE ATE PERMEATED** the carcass."*

- ❑ Corruption had **PERMEATED** every level of the government from the president to the dog catcher; they all belonged in jail.

- ❑ Before the explosion, witnesses said the smell of gasoline **PERMEATED** the flight cabin.

- ❑ Joshua was soaked clear through his raincoat; the rain had **PERMEATED** every inch of his clothing.

PERVERSE

(pur VERS) *adj.*
stubborn; contrary; intractable

Link: **REVERSE**

*"Deadwood Dick's horse was so **PERVERSE**
he often would go in **REVERSE**."*

- ❑ Our neighbor Mike is a hateful person who takes a **PERVERSE** pleasure in having the worse kept lawn in the neighborhood.

- ❑ The **PERVERSE** referee would not change his call even though the replay showed he was wrong.

- ❑ The **PERVERSENESS** of the hunting guide was apparent; he had returned to camp without us and we were lost in the woods within the hour.

PETULANT

(PEH chew lunt) *adj.*
Ill-humored, irritable, cranky

Link: **PET**

*"The **PET** you gave me made me **PETULANT**."*

- ❏ The **PETULANT** clerk slammed down her papers and stalked angrily from the office.

- ❏ The **PETULANT** old man sat on his porch and yelled at us for walking across his lawn.

- ❏ A **PETULANT** little creature, spoiled rotten by her parents, she had everything you could imagine and yet seldom ever smiled.

PHILANTHROPY

(fuh LAN thruh pee) *n.*
love of mankind, especially through
charitable gifts and deeds

Link: **PHIL ANTHROPY**

*"PHIL ANTHROPY was
a PHILANTHROPIST."*

- ❑ Football star Warrick Dunn is also known for his **PHILANTHROPY**, he helps underprivileged families own their own homes.

- ❑ In the movie, *Good Sam*, Gary Cooper's character was so **PHILANTHROPIC**, giving to anyone in need and keeping so little for his own family, that his wife left him.

- ❑ Mike is not only a real estate tycoon but he is also known as a **PHILANTHROPIST** because he gives millions to charity every year.

PHOBIA

(FOH bee uh) *n.*
a persistent, illogical fear

Link: **PHOTOS**

*"Some natives have a PHOBIA
about PHOTOS, believing their
soul will be captured inside the box."*

- ❑ Those who have a **PHOBIA** about heights are said to be acrophobic.

- ❑ Claustrophobia is the **PHOBIA** of a person who fears small, confined spaces.

- ❑ Monophobia is the **PHOBIA** of being alone.

PHOTOGENIC
(foh tuh JEN ik) *adj.*
suitable, especially attractive for photography

Link: **PHOTO GENIE**

*"The **PHOTOS** of this **PHOTOGENIC GENIE**
could get her a television series."*

- ❑ The **PHOTOGENIC** young actress posed for photographers in front of her awaiting limousine.

- ❑ The photographer couldn't stop photographing his **PHOTOGENIC** subject.

- ❑ My mother is so **PHOTOGENIC**, she always takes a good picture.

PIED

(pide) *adj.*
having patches or blotches
of two or more colors

Link: **PIED PIPER**

"If you've ever wondered where the
PIED PIPER *got his name, it*
came from wearing ***PIED*** *clothing."*

❑ The **PIED** horse was easy to spot in the race.

❑ This season's hottest Paris fashion is **PIED** skirts.

❑ The **PIED** tuxedo James wore to the ball made him the subject of much attention.

PILLAGE

(PIL luhj) *v.*
to rob of goods by violent
seizure, plunder; to take as spoils

Link: **VILLAGE**

*"Blackbeard the Pirate gives last
minute orders before they
PILLAGE the **VILLAGE**."*

❏ The enemy invaders **PILLAGED** the village,
taking everything not tied down and killing the
cows and chickens.

❏ After the kids and their school friends **PILLAGED**
the refrigerator, there was nothing left but a little
catsup and mustard.

❏ Pirates are known **PILLAGERS**.

PIQUE

(peek) *n./v.*
irritation, resentment stemming from
wounded pride; to arouse curiosity

Link: **PEEK**

*"Jo Ann was **PIQUED** at her brother for
PEEKING at her slumber party."*

- ❏ The three sisters showed their **PIQUE** at not
  being invited to their cousin's wedding by their
  refusal to send wedding presents.

- ❏ Joey said he was **PIQUED** at the chemistry
  teacher for giving out final grades before he had
  time to finish his lab work.

- ❏ The sound of the car horn **PIQUED** our curiosity
  until we saw our neighbor had accidently pressed
  it while backing out of his driveway.

VOCABULARY CARTOONS Review #24

Match the word with its definition.

___	1. periphery	a.	to rob of goods by violent seizure
___	2. permeate	b.	the outside edge
___	3. perverse	c.	to flow or spread through; penetrate
___	4. petulant	d.	love of mankind
___	5. philanthropy	e.	stubborn; contrary; intractable
___	6. phobia	f.	to arouse curiosity
___	7. photogenic	g.	suitable, attractive for photography
___	8. pied	h.	a persistent, illogical fear
___	9. pillage	i.	Ill-humored, irritable, cranky
___	10. pique	j.	having patches of two or more colors

Fill in the blanks with the most appropriate word.
The word form may need changing.

1. The _____ young actress posed for photographers in front of her awaiting limousine.

2. Colonel Mason posted guards at the _____ of the camp for night security.

3. The _____ old man sat on his porch and yelled at us for walking across his lawn.

4. The _____ referee would not change his call even though the replay showed he was wrong.

5. Football star Warrick Dunn is also known for his _____, he helps underprivileged families own their own homes.

6. Before the explosion, witnesses said the smell of gasoline _____ the flight cabin.

7. The sound of the car horn _____ our curiosity until we saw our neighbor had accidently pressed it while backing out of his driveway.

8. The _____ horse was easy to spot in the race.

9. The enemy invaders _____ the village, taking everything not tied down and killing the cows and chickens.

10. Those who have a _____ about heights are said to be acrophobic.

278

PLIGHT

(plite) *n.*
a condition of a situation,
especially a distressing one

Link: **FLIGHT**

*"A **PLIGHT** in **FLIGHT**."*

- ❏ In most dramatic stage plays, the **PLIGHT** of the good guys appears at its worse at the end of the second act.

- ❏ Determined to rescue the fifty hostages from their **PLIGHT**, the police rushed the aircraft before the terrorists could cause further harm.

- ❏ Christopher's friend advised him not to worsen the **PLIGHT** he had gotten himself into by starting a fight, which could only make matters worse.

PORCINE

(POOR sine) *adj.*
reminiscent of or pertaining
to a pig; resembling a pig

Link: **POOR SCENE**

*"It was a **POOR SCENE** when Mark
arrived with his **PORCINE** date."*

- ❏ After an around the world cruise, where each meal is a grand feast, Bob and Helen returned home with **PORCINE** figures.

- ❏ She had a **PORCINE** attitude about food, that is to say, she would eat anything and everything.

- ❏ In order to endure the **PORCINE** smell of the pig sty, Frank tied a bandana around his head to cover his nose.

Link: **IMPORTANT TATER**

*"A **POTENTATE** in 'Tater Kingdom' is
an **IMPORTANT TATER**."*

- ❏ **POTENTATES** are usually not elected officials, but the descendants of a line of rajahs, sheiks, or kings.

- ❏ The Shah of Iran was an Iranian **POTENTATE** who lived in the twentieth century.

- ❏ Ever since Sarah was elected president of the junior class, she walks around with her nose in the air, as if she thinks she is a **POTENTATE**.

PRECARIOUS

(pruh KARE ee us) *adj.*
unsafe, unsteady, unstable

Link: **CARRY US**

*"To escape the dinosaur, Mississippi
Jones **CARRIED US** to safety
across a **PRECARIOUS** bridge."*

❑ John was scared to climb the **PRECARIOUS** ladder because he didn't want to fall and break his back.

❑ The **PRECARIOUSNESS** of their situation did not fully strike the fishermen until their small boat arrived at the dock only moments before the storm struck.

❑ Isabel's habit of arriving at work late almost every morning made her job future **PRECARIOUSLY** uncertain.

PROCRASTINATE
(proh KRAS tuh nayt) *v.*
to put off until a later time

Link: **GRASS HATE**

*"Larry **HATED** to cut the **GRASS** and would
PROCRASTINATE about it for weeks."*

- ❑ Never do today what you can **PROCRASTINATE**
  doing until tomorrow, a famous husband once
  said.

- ❑ Laura received a bad grade on her science project
  because she **PROCRASTINATED** finishing it until
  the day before it was due.

- ❑ Wilcox had a **PROCRASTINATING** personality;
  whatever he started, you felt he was probably not
  going to finish.

PROFICIENT
(pruh FISH unt) *adj.*
skillful; to be very good at something

Link: **PRO FISHERMAN**

*"The ultimate **PROFICIENT PRO FISHERMAN**"*

- ❑ Wally was the most **PROFICIENT** tennis player in our league, but he wasn't good enough to win the regional tournament.

- ❑ June was so **PROFICIENT** as executive secretary, she was promoted and became vice president of sales.

- ❑ Dad finally gave up trying to install the ceiling fan and asked mom to find someone who was more **PROFICIENT**.

PROPULSIVE
(PROH pul siv) *adj.*
the act or process of propelling;
a propelling force

Link: **PROPELLER**

*"**PROPELLERS** provide the **PROPULSIVE** force that **PROPEL** many transportation vehicles."*

- ❑ The first ship **PROPELLED** by a **PROPELLER** was invented by Isambard Brunel in 1844.

- ❑ Physically pumping the pedals creates the needed **PROPULSIVE** force to power a bicycle.

- ❑ The **PROPULSIVE** force of a nuclear submarine is superior to the older diesel powered submarines.

PROWESS

(PROW iss) *n.*
exceptional skill and bravery

Link: **PROWLER**

*"The **PROWESS** of a **PROWLER**"*

- ❏ The **PROWESS** of the Sioux chief, Crazy Horse, at leading his warriors into battle, was legendary.

- ❏ Rod Laver's **PROWESS** as the world's best tennis player in the history of the game is supported by the fact that he won the Grand Slam twice. This has not been done since.

- ❏ Because of his **PROWESS** in battle, Brad was awarded the silver star.

QUANDARY
(KWAHN dree) *n.*
state of perplexity or doubt; a
difficult or uncertain situation

Link: **LAUNDRY**

*"A **QUANDARY** in the **LAUNDRY**"*

___

❑ The police were in a **QUANDARY**; the butler's
fingerprints were all over the murder weapon, but
he was two thousand miles away and appearing
on the *Tonight Show* during the time the murder
was committed.

❑ Andrea was in a **QUANDARY**. She was asked to
the prom by two boys she really liked.

❑ Bob's **QUANDARY** was to get married and move
out of town or stay in his home town where he
really wants to live.

QUEUE
(kyoo) *v./n.*
to form or to wait in line; a line

Link: **Q**

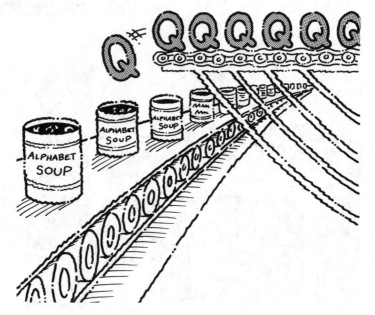

"Qs in a QUEUE"

- ❑ During the Wimbledon Tennis Championships, fans **QUEUE** outside the gates the day before and spend the night waiting for the gates to open the following morning.

- ❑ The sisters decided not to attend the movie because a line was **QUEUING** up as they arrived, and they didn't want to stand in a **QUEUE** in the cold, night air.

- ❑ The **QUEUES** at Disney World are usually the longest during holiday weekends.

VOCABULARY CARTOONS Review #25

Match the word with its definition.

___ 1. plight
___ 2. porcine
___ 3. potentate
___ 4. precarious
___ 5. procrastinate
___ 6. proficient
___ 7. propulsive
___ 8. prowess
___ 9. quandary
___ 10. queue

a. a powerful ruler; an important person
b. to put off until a later time
c. unsafe, unsteady, unstable
d. a condition of a distressing situation
e. exceptional skill and bravery
f. to form or to wait in line; a line
g. resembling a pig
h. a difficult or uncertain situation
i. the act or process of propelling
j. skillful; to be very good at something

Fill in the blanks with the most appropriate word. The word form may need changing.

1. Because of his _____ in battle, Brad was awarded the silver star.

2. Laura received a bad grade on her science project because she _____ finishing it until the day before it was due.

3. The _____ at Disney World are usually the longest during holiday weekends.

4. John was scared to climb the _____ ladder because he didn't want to fall and break his back.

5. Andrea was in a _____. She was asked to the prom by two boys she really liked.

6. Ever since Sarah was elected president of the junior class, she walks around with her nose in the air, as if she thinks she is a _____.

7. The _____ force of a nuclear submarine is superior to the older diesel powered submarines.

8. In order to endure the _____ smell of the pig sty, Frank tied a bandana around his head to cover his nose.

9. Wally was the most _____ tennis player in our league, but he wasn't good enough to win the regional tournament.

10. Determined to rescue the fifty hostages from their _____, the police rushed the aircraft before the terrorists could cause further harm.

289

QUIRK
(kwurk) *n.*
a peculiarity of behavior; an
unaccountable act or event

Link: **JERK**

*"People have the strangest QUIRKS;
some can be real JERKS."*

- ❑ Watch out for this horse's **QUIRK**; he bucks every time he sneezes.

- ❑ Bryan has the weirdest **QUIRK**; he chews his tongue whenever he is in deep thought.

- ❑ It was a **QUIRK** of fate that Elizabeth was sick at home the day her car pool had an accident.

QUIXOTIC
(kwik SAHT ik) *adj.*
totally or foolishly impractical

Link: **IDIOTIC**

"Jim, the messenger, is not
***IDIOTIC**, he's just **QUIXOTIC**."*

- ❏ Sally's **QUIXOTIC** dream was that a prince riding a white stallion would someday scoop her up and ask her to marry him.

- ❏ Putting all taxpayers on the honor system is a **QUIXOTIC** suggestion.

- ❏ Sue had the most **QUIXOTIC** ideas of what her life would be like if she ever won the lottery.

Note: *The word quixotic derives from an ancient Spanish novel in which the hero, Don Quixote, is idealistic to an impractical degree.*

RAMIFICATION

(ram uh fuh KAY shun) *n.*
a development growing out of and often
complicating a problem or pain; a consequence

Link: **RAMS ON VACATION**

*"A possible **RAMIFICATION** of
encountering **RAMS** while **ON VACATION**"*

- ❑ Courtney did not realize that being late for work three mornings in a row would have **RAMIFICATIONS** until her boss fired her.

- ❑ The **RAMIFICATION** of not studying for a test is the high probability of failing it.

- ❑ A **RAMIFICATION** is a development or consequence that grows from the main body as limbs grow from trees and plants; therefore, there are **RAMIFICATIONS** to every act a person makes no matter how small, because every act has a consequence.

RELINQUISH

(rah LING kwish) *v.*
to give up doing, professing, or
intending; to surrender, give in

Link: **REEL IN FISH**

*"Captain Ahab would never **RELINQUISH**
REELING IN the **FISH**."*

- ❏ I will never **RELINQUISH** my ambition to play professional football.

- ❏ Bobby would not **RELINQUISH** his bag of Halloween candy and fell asleep with it clutched in his arms.

- ❏ The retiring CEO merrily **RELINQUISHED** his control of the company with a wave of his hand as he stood on his yacht.

REMINISCE

(rem uh NISS) *v.*
the act or practice
of recalling the past

Link: **RIM MISS**

*"Jim never got over his **RIM MISS** and tortured
himself for years **REMINISCING** about it."*

- ❏ Sometimes when we are feeling nostalgic, my
  wife and I lie back and listen to the music of the
  1980s and **REMINISCE** about when we were
  dating and the things we used to do.

- ❏ The **REMINISCENT** qualities in his art brought
  back fond memories of Paris in the 19th century.

- ❏ After my mother died, it was hard not to
  REMINISCE about all the great times we had
  together.

REMORSE
(re MORS) *n.*
a strong feeling of sadness or guilt
for having done something wrong

Link: **HORSE**

*"The **HORSE** felt **REMORSE**."*

- ❏ John refused to feel any **REMORSE** for doing what he considered the right thing to do.

- ❏ The **REMORSE** we feel for hurting those we love is the beginning of being able to say we're sorry.

- ❏ When the pall bearers came forward with the casket, the widow let out a **REMORSEFUL** sob.

RESURGENT
(re SUR jent) *adj.*
rising after defeat

Link: **SERGEANT**

"A RESURGENT SERGEANT"

- ❑ After failing math the last two years, the **RESURGENT** young boy studied diligently and passed with an A.

- ❑ The **RESURGENT** little boy was determined to ride his bike without training wheels.

- ❑ **RESURGENCE** and strong determination helps most climbers conquer Mount Everest.

REVERE

(ruh VEER) *v.*
to regard with great devotion
or respect, to honor

Link: **PAUL REVERE**

"Hero of the American Revolution,
***PAUL REVERE** is greatly **REVERED**."*

❑ Mother Teresa was greatly **REVERED** by all who knew of her humanitarian work in Africa.

❑ Another who enjoyed almost universal recognition and **REVERENCE** for his humanitarianism in the medical field was Dr. Schweitzer.

❑ Everyone **REVERES** Father Monahan; he is such a good and kindhearted pastor.

RIVET
(RIV it) *v./n.*
to hold the attention of; something
that fastens two parts together

Link: **RIVET**

*"The audience was **RIVETED** to their
seats watching the **RIVETER**."*

- ❏ Some actors have a certain charisma; once they
  appear on stage all eyes are **RIVETED** upon
  them.

- ❏ The home crowd was **RIVETED** as their player
  stood at the foul line ready to shoot the winning
  basket.

- ❏ Most naval ships, army tanks, and fighter aircraft
  have metal plates for their outer bodies that are
  held together by **RIVETS**.

ROSTER

(RAW ster) *n.*
a list of names; especially of
personnel available for duty

Link: **ROOSTER**

*"A **ROOSTER** on the **ROSTER**"*

- ❏ The football program has a **ROSTER** for both teams with the player's jersey numbers and positions.

- ❏ Tom saw his name on the duty **ROSTER**.

- ❏ The military is full of all types of **ROSTERS**; there is a duty **ROSTER**, a leave **ROSTER,** and even a **ROSTER** for standing guard.

Match the word with its definition.

__	1. quirk	a.	a consequence
__	2. quixotic	b.	a strong feeling of sadness or guilt
__	3. ramification	c.	a list of names
__	4. relinquish	d.	rising after defeat
__	5. reminisce	e.	the act or practice of recalling the past
__	6. remorse	f.	to hold the attention of
__	7. resurgent	g.	to honor
__	8. revere	h.	a peculiarity of behavior
__	9. rivet	i.	to give up doing, to surrender, give in
__	10. roster	j.	totally or foolishly impractical

Fill in the blanks with the most appropriate word. The word form may need changing.

1. John refused to feel any _____ for doing what he considered the right thing to do.

2. The _____ of not studying for a test is the high probability of failing it.

3. The football program has a _____ for both teams with the player's jersey numbers and positions.

4. Watch out for this horse's _____; he bucks every time he sneezes.

5. Sally's _____ dream was that a prince riding a white stallion would someday scoop her up and ask her to marry him.

6. The home crowd was _____ as their player stood at the foul line ready to shoot the winning basket.

7. Bobby would not _____ his bag of Halloween candy and fell asleep with it clutched in his arms.

8. After failing math the last two years, the _____ young boy studied diligently and passed with an A.

9. After my mother died, it was hard not to _____ about all the great times we had together.

10. Mother Teresa was greatly _____ by all who knew of her humanitarian work in Africa.

300

RUDIMENTARY
(roo duh MEN tuh ree) *adj.*
basic, crude, undeveloped;
fundamental principles or skills

Link: **RUDE ELEMENTARY**

*"RUDE children in **ELEMENTARY** school
are often **RUDIMENTARY** by nature."*

- ❏ **"RUDIMENTARY**, my dear Watson," Sherlock Holmes used to say to Dr. Watson when he had uncovered an important clue to a murder.

- ❏ If Tarzan lived with apes all his life, his social skills must have been very **RUDIMENTARY**.

- ❏ The eating utensils and tools of early cave dwellers during the Ice Age were very **RUDIMENTARY**.

SCAPEGOAT
(SCAPE goht) *n.*
one that bears the blame for others

Link: **GOAT**

*"I ask you, does this **GOAT** look
like a **SCAPEGOAT**?"*

- ❑ Mary said she was not one of the sorority sisters
  who stayed out late, and she wasn't going to be
  the **SCAPEGOAT** for the ones who did.

- ❑ Poor Henry was always the **SCAPEGOAT**,
  taking blame for whatever happened, whether he
  was to blame or not.

- ❑ I told Sam that I wasn't going to be the **SCAPE-
  GOAT**; he was the one who broke the window,
  not me.

SCRUTINIZE
(SKROOT uh nize) *v.*
to look very carefully; to examine

Link: **SCREW EYES**

*"U.S. Customs officials have **SCREW
EYES** when they **SCRUTINIZE** baggage."*

- ❏ Newspaper proofreaders **SCRUTINIZE** an entire newspaper each day.

- ❏ Each soldier's uniform is **SCRUTINIZED** by his commanding officer.

- ❏ I **SCRUTINIZED** all the books in the library and found several I had wanted.

SEGREGATE
(SEG ruh gate) *v.*
to separate or keep apart from others

Link: **SEPARATE GATE**

*"At the track, race horses are **SEGREGATED** into
SEPARATE GATES to begin the race."*

- ❑ The cattleman built a fence to **SEGREGATE** the bulls from the heifers.

- ❑ To **SEGREGATE** truth from fiction is the duty and obligation of every trial jury.

- ❑ The chairman asked the board to **SEGREGATE** the facts from the rumors so they could arrive at a reasonable course of action.

SERPENTINE
(sur pun TEEN) *adj.*
snakelike in shape or
movement; winding as a snake

Link: **SERPENT TEEN**

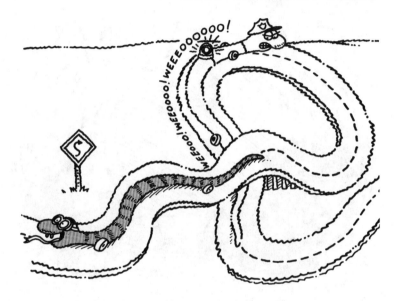

*"A **SERPENT TEEN** hot-rodding
on a **SERPENTINE** road"*

❑ The **SERPENTINE** race track was a challenging course for the drivers, especially in the rain.

❑ Really good mystery stories have **SERPENTINE** plots that lead the reader first one way, then back another, always keeping you guessing to the very end.

❑ The quarterback dashed through the line, **SERPENTINING** his way through tacklers until he scored the winning touchdown.

SOMBER

(SOM bur) *adj.*
depressing, gloomy, dark

Link: **SOME BEARS**

*"**SOME BEARS** endure winter
hibernation in a **SOMBER** state of mind."*

❑ You will find most everyone who attends a
funeral wears **SOMBER** clothing, generally
black or gray.

❑ He had the most **SOMBER** expression, and
there was nothing we could do to cheer him up,
hardly what one might expect from a man getting
married the next day.

❑ The **SOMBER** weather forecast spoiled our
weekend plans to go to the beach.

SONOROUS

(SON uh russ) adj.
producing sound, especially
deep and rich, resonant

Link: **SNORERS**

*"The not-so-**SONOROUS**
SNORERS of old Santa Fe"*

- ❏ John Barrymore's **SONOROUS** voice enraptured audiences across the land for decades.

- ❏ The **SONORITY** of the school choir as they sang Christmas carols in the auditorium was uplifting and delightfully spiritual.

- ❏ The **SONOROUS** drums from the band could be heard from outside the stadium.

SPUR
(spur) *v.*
to move to action

Link: **SPURS**

*"**SPURS** are called **SPURS** because
they **SPUR** a horse to action."*

- ❑ The coach told his players that his job was not only to teach, but to **SPUR** them on to do their best.

- ❑ The general **SPURRED** his troops to make one last effort to take the hill.

- ❑ The principal's talk on good citizenship **SPURRED** the students into not littering the school grounds.

Link: **BURN**

*"Robert was **BURNED** when Rebecca **SPURNED** him."*

❑ James talked of nothing but how much he wanted a date with Ruth, but would never ask her for fear she would **SPURN** him.

❑ The buyer's ridiculously low offer to buy the house was **SPURNED** by the seller.

❑ When Jimmy Connors won the tennis match and offered to shake hands with his opponent, the loser **SPURNED** Jimmy's hand and walked off.

STUPEFY

(STOO puh fie) *v.*
to make numb with amazement;
to stun into helplessness

Link: **SUPER FLY**

*"The kids were **STUPEFIED**
when **SUPER FLY** stole the cake."*

- ❑ When Corporal Burch heard that an atomic bomb had been dropped on Japan and the war was over, he was **STUPEFIED**.

- ❑ The magician's trick left his audience **STUPEFIED**.

- ❑ The plumber seemed **STUPEFIED** when he could not fix the leaky faucet.

Match the word with its definition.

___	1. rudimentary	a. to move to action
___	2. scapegoat	b. depressing, gloomy, dark
___	3. scrutinize	c. to keep apart from others
___	4. segregate	d. to make numb with amazement
___	5. serpentine	e. snakelike in shape or movement
___	6. somber	f. to reject with disdain
___	7. sonorous	g. basic, fundamental skills
___	8. spur	h. to look very carefully; to examine
___	9. spurn	i. producing deep and rich sound
___	10. stupefy	j. one that bears the blame for others

Fill in the blanks with the most appropriate word.
The word form may need changing.

1. The _____ race track was a challenging course for the drivers, especially in the rain.

2. The cattleman built a fence to _____ the bulls from the heifers.

3. The _____ weather forecast spoiled our weekend plans to go to the beach.

4. Each soldier's uniform is _____ by his commanding officer.

5. I told Sam that I wasn't going to be his _____; he was the one who broke the window, not me.

6. John Barrymore's _____ voice enraptured audiences across the land for decades.

7. The magician's trick left his audience _____.

8. The buyer's ridiculously low offer to buy the house was _____ by the seller.

9. The eating utensils and tools of early cave dwellers during the Ice Age were very _____.

10. The general _____ his troops to make one last effort to take the hill.

SUNDRY

(SUN dree) *adj.*
various, several, miscellaneous

Link: **SUNDAE**

*"Jimmy had a **SUNDRY** of ice cream
SUNDAES for his birthday."*

❑ A **SUNDRY** store is usually like a five and dime,
   a store carrying a variety of miscellaneous items
   for the household and personal use.

❑ **SUNDRY** articles in the newspaper written by
   parents and politicians would have you believe
   our school system leaves a lot to be desired.

❑ You can find **SUNDRY** tools in my dad's tool
   box.

SUPPLANT
(suh PLANT) *v.*
to take the place of

Link: **PLANT**

*"Gardeners **PLANT** new plants to*
***SUPPLANT** old **PLANTS**."*

- After the school superintendent retired, she was **SUPPLANTED** by the deputy superintendent.

- The Recreation and Parks Department's proposed budget for next year was quickly **SUPPLANTED** by a budget mandated by the Board of County Commissioners.

- After the starting quarterback threw three interceptions in the first half, the coach **SUPPLANTED** him with the second string quarterback in the second half.

SURFEIT

(SUR fit) *n.*
an overabundant amount, especially
overindulgence in eating and drinking

Link: **SURFERS**

*"A **SURFEIT** of **SURFERS** is a sure path to
disastrous surfboard accidents."*

- There was a **SURFEIT** of delicious food at the family picnic.

- The beach store had a **SURFEIT** of bathing suits and last Saturday put on a bathing suit sale.

- A **SURFEIT** of recruits showed up to try out for the team, and Coach Rex had to turn the freshmen away.

TETHER

(TEH thur) *n.*
a rope or chain that allows limited movement;
the limit of one's resources or strength

Link: **LEATHER**

*"Horses are **TETHERED** with a
rope or **LEATHER** strap."*

❏ Norman told the guys that he had too much work
to go camping, but we knew it was because his
wife had him **TETHERED** to a short leash and
wouldn't let him go.

❏ We **TETHERED** the boat to the dock with lines
both fore and aft.

❏ The prisoners were **TETHERED** by heavy
chains in groups of three.

TORQUE

(tork) *n.*
a turning or twisting force

Link: **TURK**

*"Tommy the **TURK** doing his
famous **TORQUE TURK** dance"*

❑ We all took our turn, but none of my brothers or I
could apply enough **TORQUE** to open the jar of
strawberry jam.

❑ When the propeller broke off one side, this created
a **TORQUE** so great it tore the engine right out of
its mount.

❑ The wrench handle was too short to generate the
TORQUE required to loosen the bolt.

TRENCHANT

(TREN chunt) *adj.*
cutting, incisive, having a sharp
point; caustic, sarcastic

Link: **TRENCH ANT**

*"A **TRENCHANT** mouth is characteristic of the
famous Madagascar **TRENCH ANT**."*

- ❏ Roger's remarks at the budget meeting were
  TRENCHANT, because he knew precisely where
  the financial problems lay.

- ❏ The music teacher made numerous **TRENCHANT**
  comments about the band's performance; clearly
  she thought the band stunk.

- ❏ Julia had a **TRENCHANT** tongue and was always
  putting her friends down behind their backs.

TRUCULENT

(TRUH kyoo lunt) *adj.*
inclined toward conflict; eager to fight

Link: **TRUCK YOU LENT**

*"The **TRUCK YOU LENT** Uncle Frank
made him **TRUCULENT**."*

❏ Looking back on it, we never understood what
made Randolph **TRUCULENT** all through school;
he always had a chip on his shoulder.

❏ A **TRUCULENT** attitude seldom wins friends or
influences people in a positive way.

❏ The marine recruits were scolded by their
TRUCULENT sergeant for any small offense.

TRUNCATE
(TRUNG kayt) *v.*
to shorten by cutting off

Link: **TRUNK CUT**

*"The lumberjack **TRUNCATED** the tree when he made a **TRUNK CUT** halfway to the top."*

☐ Observing that his listeners were falling asleep, the president **TRUNCATED** his speech so everyone could go home.

☐ Because of unforeseen circumstances, our vacation was **TRUNCATED** after the first week.

☐ We **TRUNCATED** the brush around our house so we could have a better view of the lake.

TYRO
(TY row) *n.*
a beginner; a novice

Link: **TIE ROPE**

*"You could tell by the way Curly TIED
ROPE, that he was a cowboy TYRO."*

- ❑ People never suspected that this was Henry's first marathon race; he ran the course like a veteran instead of a **TYRO**.

- ❑ What the forest rangers hated most was the 4th of July and other national holidays when hordes of camping **TYROS** invaded the park and littered the forest, all of which had to be cleaned after they departed.

- ❑ When it comes to cooking, Bob is such a **TYRO**, he can't even boil water without making a mess.

UBIQUITOUS

(yoo BIK wih tus) *adj.*
existing or being everywhere at the same
time; constantly encountered; widespread

Link: **BIG AS US**

*"When you're as **BIG AS US**
you feel **UBIQUITOUS**."*

- ❑ Computers were once rare, but today are more **UBIQUITOUS** than typewriters.

- ❑ The **UBIQUITY** of fast-food restaurants around the world has become an established fact.

- ❑ Cowboy boots are as **UBIQUITOUS** as blue jeans at a rodeo.

VOCABULARY CARTOONS Review #28

Match the word with its definition.

___	1. sundry	a.	an overabundant amount
___	2. supplant	b.	being everywhere at the same time
___	3. surfeit	c.	a beginner; a novice
___	4. tether	d.	various, several, miscellaneous
___	5. torque	e.	a rope that allows limited movement
___	6. trenchant	f.	a turning or twisting force
___	7. truculent	g.	to shorten by cutting off
___	8. truncate	h.	cutting, having a sharp point; sarcastic
___	9. tyro	i.	inclined toward conflict; eager to fight
___ 10.	ubiquitous	j.	to take the place of

Fill in the blanks with the most appropriate word.
The word form may need changing.

1. We _____ the boat to the dock with lines both fore and aft.

2. The wrench handle was too short to generate the _____ required to loosen the bolt.

3. Because of unforeseen circumstances, our vacation was _____ after the first week.

4. There was a _____ of delicious food at the family picnic.

5. A _____ store is usually like a five and dime, a store carrying a variety of miscellaneous items for the household and personal use.

6. After the starting quarterback threw three interceptions in the first half the coach _____ him with the second string quarterback in the second half.

7. Julia had a _____ tongue and was always putting her friends down behind their backs.

8. The marine recruits were scolded by their _____ sergeant for any small offense.

9. Computers were once rare, but today are more _____ than typewriters.

10. When it comes to cooking, Bob is such a _____, he can't even boil water without making a mess.

UMBRAGE

(UM brij) *n.*
sense of injury or insult; to
take offense, displeasure

Link: **DUMB BRIDGE**

*"Mike, the engineer, took **UMBRAGE** when
people called it a **DUMB BRIDGE**."*

❑ Polly took **UMBRAGE** when her husband told her
she was wearing too much makeup and looked
older than she was by trying to look younger than
she was.

❑ "I take **UMBRAGE** at your remarks about my golf
game," Theodore said jokingly to his regular golf
partner. "I'm the only one you can beat."

❑ Please don't take **UMBRAGE** of my criticisms, I
am only trying to tell the truth.

UNBRIDLED
(un BRIDE duld) *adj.*
violent, unbounded, unrestrained

Link: **BRIDLE**

*"A wild horse without a **BRIDLE** can
be an **UNBRIDLED** demon to ride."*

❑ It is small wonder the children in that family are
always in trouble; they are **UNBRIDLED** and do
whatever they please.

❑ In last-minute desperation, the candidate made
an **UNBRIDLED** speech full of deceitful
accusations he hoped would discredit the mayor.

❑ Andrea's **UNBRIDLED** passion for dancing was
evident in every performance she gave.

Link: **PIER**

*"Vern, I told you to **VEER**
at the end of the **PIER**."*

❏ When you arrive at the castle, **VEER** left around the wall and follow the foot trail until you come to the valley.

❏ Without warning, Flight #638 suddenly **VEERED** off the runway and slammed into a small plane parked outside the hanger. Fortunately no one was seriously hurt.

❏ Arthur never **VEERED** from the path of honor and dignity.

VERBATIM

(ver BAY tum) *n.*
using exactly the same
words, word for word

Link: **VERN'S BAT**

*"**VERN** wrote his coach's batting
instructions **VERBATIM** on his **BAT**."*

❏ The coach called the team together and said
from that moment on, every player who wanted
to stay on the team had to obey his rules
VERBATIM.

❏ The young actress had a tough time learning her
lines **VERBATIM**.

❏ Polly, the parrot, will repeat whatever is said to
him **VERBATIM**.

VERTIGO
(VUR tuh go) *n.*
the sensation of dizziness

Link: **WHERE TO GO**

"When test pilot Bill developed a bad case of VERTIGO, he didn't know WHERE TO GO."

- Charles was acrophobic and even suffered from **VERTIGO** while standing on a stool, replacing the lights in the kitchen.

- A person said to have acrophobia is someone who has a fear of great heights. Typically, acrophobes suffer from **VERTIGO** if they are in a tall building and look down.

- Dad said he couldn't ride any of the amusement park rides that spin because they gave him **VERTIGO**.

VOLITION
(voh LISH un) *n.*
an act of choosing, using one's
own will in a conscious choice

Link: **GO FISHIN'**

*"Of his own **VOLITION**, Bryan would
have preferred to **GO FISHIN'**."*

❑ Mom was surprised when Laura ordered a veggie
sandwich of her own **VOLITION**; she normally
despises vegetables.

❑ Dave decided to join the Army of his own
VOLITION in lieu of going to college.

❑ The dean asked Peter if he was joining a
fraternity because of peer pressure or of his own
VOLITION.

WANE

(wayn) *v.*
to decrease gradually

Link: **RAIN**

*"Snowmen **WANE** in the **RAIN**."*

- ❑ Marilyn's interest in a new beau began to **WANE** when she discovered Jack had invited three other girls as his date for the junior prom.

- ❑ With a **WANING** of air in his air tank, the diver knew he had to return to the surface.

- ❑ A **WANING** interest by theater-goers prompted the theater to shut down.

WITHER
(WITH ur) *v./adj.*
to become dry; shriveled, shrunken, dried-up

Link: **WEATHER**

"Too much sun and too little rain makes corn
***WITHER** in the summer **WEATHER**."*

- ❑ The crop **WITHERED** from the lack of rain.

- ❑ A few **WITHERED** apples were all that remained on the tree after the pickers had worked their way through the orchard.

- ❑ He remembered her as a bouncy cheerleader. Fifty years later he attended his high school reunion, only to find she was still bouncy, but a bit **WITHERED** with the passage of time.

WREST

(rest) *v.*
to pull away, take by violence

Link: **WRIST**

"The policeman grabbed the thief by the
***WRIST** and **WRESTED** away his gun."*

- ❏ Police will tell you that in dealing with a person who threatens you with a knife or a club, it is the best policy not to attempt to **WREST** the weapon away from them.

- ❏ When it was clear that the driver had too much to drink, the passengers **WRESTED** the keys away from him for their own safety.

- ❏ The excited puppy **WRESTED** the stick from the boy's hand.

YORE
(yohr) *n.*
former days, an era long past

Link: **FLOOR**

*"In days of YORE, folks
slept on the FLOOR."*

- ❏ (**YORE** is generally to be seen in the phrase "days of **YORE**.") In days of **YORE**, my sister and I had to walk five miles to school in waist-deep snow.

- ❏ In the days of **YORE** we didn't have the luxuries of air-conditioning, televisions and home computers.

- ❏ An exception to the word yore meaning a time long past would be the Royal House of **YORE**, which held the English throne from 1461 to 1485. But that of course, was in the days of **YORE**.

VOCABULARY CARTOONS Review #29

Match the word with its definition.

___ 1. umbrage   a. to become dry; shriveled
___ 2. unbridled   b. to pull away, take by violence
___ 3. veer   c. using exactly the same words
___ 4. verbatim   d. sense of insult; to take offense
___ 5. vertigo   e. former days, an era long past
___ 6. volition   f. violent, unbounded, unrestrained
___ 7. wane   g. to change direction
___ 8. wither   h. an act of choosing
___ 9. wrest   i. to decrease gradually
___ 10. yore   j. the sensation of dizziness

Fill in the blanks with the most appropriate word. The word form may need changing.

1. Polly, the parrot, will repeat whatever is said to him _____.

2. The crop _____ from the lack of rain.

3. Police will tell you that in dealing with a person who threatens you with a knife or a club, it is the best policy not to attempt to _____ the weapon away from them.

4. Andrea's _____ passion for dancing was evident in every performance she gave.

5. Dad said he couldn't ride any of the amusement park rides that spin because they gave him _____.

6. Without warning, Flight #638 suddenly _____ off the runway and slammed into a small plane parked outside the hanger.

7. In the days of _____ we didn't have the luxuries of air-conditioning, televisions and home computers.

8. Polly took _____ when her husband told her she was wearing too much makeup and looked older than she was by trying to look younger than she was.

9. Dave decided to join the Army of his own _____ in lieu of going to college.

10. A _____ interest by theater-goers prompted the theater to shut down.

333

Review Answers

REVIEW #1, page 25
Matching:
1. (d or i)
2. (d or i)
3. g
4. a
5. f
6. c
7. j
8. h
9. b
10. e

Fill in the Blank:
1. abuts
2. abridged
3. abhors or abominates
4. affidavit
5. abyss
6. abhor or abominate
7. affinity
8. accolades
9. adjunct
10. abstruse

REVIEW #2, page 36
Matching:
1. b
2. h
3. c
4. a
5. f
6. i
7. j
8. g
9. e
10. d

Fill in the Blank:
1. alienated
2. also-ran
3. aggrandize
4. altercation
5. allured
6. aftermath
7. alternative
8. ajar
9. aloof
10. alleviates

REVIEW #3, page 47
Matching:
1. d
2. e
3. c
4. f
5. j
6. b
7. h
8. a
9. g
10. i

Fill in the Blank:
1. antecedent
2. ambiance
3. aptitude
4. amenable
5. artisans
6. arduous
7. anterior
8. amplified
9. archaic
10. appalled

REVIEW #4, page 58

Matching:
1. f
2. j
3. e
4. h
5. c
6. g
7. i
8. b
9. a
10. d

Fill in the Blank:
1. aspired
2. austere
3. asunder
4. atypical
5. assuage
6. badgered
7. askew
8. astute
9. ballistics
10. atrophied

REVIEW #5, page 69

Matching:
1. d
2. j
3. (a or b)
4. i
5. (a or b)
6. h
7. e
8. f
9. c
10. g

Fill in the Blank:
1. blather
2. bizarre
3. bereaved
4. balmy
5. bludgeon
6. bucolic
7. bleak
8. beleaguered
9. beget
10. beset

REVIEW #6, page 80

Matching:
1. f
2. h
3. c
4. g
5. e
6. d
7. j
8. i
9. a
10. b

Fill in the Blank:
1. capacious
2. callow
3. cajoled
4. castigated
5. cache
6. candor
7. cacophony
8. catapulted
9. callous
10. bulwark

REVIEW #7, page 91

Matching:
1. j
2. c
3. e
4. b
5. i
6. a
7. h
8. d
9. g
10. f

Fill in the Blank:
1. cerebral
2. chronic
3. catharsis
4. chattel
5. chided
6. caucus
7. circa
8. certified
9. citadels
10. chasm

REVIEW #8, page 102

Matching:
1. i
2. h
3. d
4. f
5. g
6. j
7. b
8. c
9. a
10. e

Fill in the Blank:
1. commodious
2. claimants
3. comprised
4. consensus
5. congenial
6. coterie
7. countenance
8. coup
9. cloister
10. connoisseur

REVIEW #9, page 113

Matching:
1. e
2. b
3. a
4. f
5. i
6. c
7. j
8. d
9. g
10. h

Fill in the Blank:
1. cowered
2. damper
3. cranny
4. curtailed
5. cubism
6. couture
7. curvilinear
8. creditors
9. criterion
10. craven

REVIEW #10, page 124

Matching:	Fill in the Blank:
1. e	1. deft
2. g	2. dauntless
3. a	3. demonic
4. h	4. dearth
5. d	5. decree
6. j	6. demagogues
7. i	7. defamed
8. f	8. debasing
9. b	9. debacle
10. c	10. deduced

REVIEW #11, page 135

Matching:	Fill in the Blank:
1. b	1. desiccated
2. (e or i)	2. dissolution
3. a	3. disperse
4. g	4. denounced or disparaged
5. (e or i)	5. disparaging or denouncing
6. c	6. dispel
7. h	7. dilemma
8. d	8. docile
9. j	9. divine
10. f	10. demur

REVIEW #12, page 146

Matching:	Fill in the Blank:
1. b	1. duress
2. f	2. domain
3. h	3. doldrums
4. g	4. dulcet
5. a	5. dormant
6. e	6. effaced
7. j	7. egalitarian
8. i	8. edifice
9. c	9. dromedaries
10. d	10. draconian

REVIEW #13, page 157

Matching:
1. b
2. a
3. c
4. d
5. j
6. i
7. e
8. h
9. f
10. g

Fill in the Blank:
1. emitted
2. endured
3. elfin
4. engulfed
5. elapsed
6. emulate
7. enraged
8. embellished
9. enraptured
10. embodied

REVIEW #14, page 168

Matching:
1. c
2. e
3. a
4. f
5. g
6. d
7. b
8. h
9. j
10. i

Fill in the Blank:
1. evaded
2. evoke
3. enticed
4. exhume
5. euphonious
6. erudite
7. entomologists
8. ensemble
9. entreated
10. entombed

REVIEW #15, page 179

Matching:
1. j
2. i
3. h
4. a
5. g
6. b
7. f
8. c
9. e
10. d

Fill in the Blank:
1. fleeced
2. fickle
3. fawned
4. expunged
5. facilitate
6. fetish
7. fathom
8. feigned
9. festering
10. fjords

REVIEW #16, page 190
Matching:
1. i
2. (f or h)
3. (f or h)
4. d
5. a
6. e
7. g
8. j
9. c
10. b

Fill in the Blank:
1. giddy
2. foraging
3. fraught
4. generalizing
5. gamin
6. gazebo
7. fortuitous
8. girded
9. forbear or forsake
10. forbear or forsake

REVIEW #17, page 201
Matching:
1. j
2. f
3. b
4. i
5. e
6. c
7. a
8. h
9. g
10. d

Fill in the Blank:
1. gossamer
2. guise
3. guile
4. gluttons
5. girth
6. gloated
7. grandiloquent
8. harrowing
9. harangued
10. grandiose

REVIEW #18, page 212
Matching:
1. b
2. c
3. f
4. h
5. g
6. d
7. a
8. i
9. j
10. e

Fill in the Blank:
1. idiosyncrasy
2. hovels
3. incites
4. hoard
5. infamous
6. incongruous
7. histrionic
8. husbandry
9. herbicide
10. impeded

REVIEW #19, page 223

Matching:	Fill in the Blank:
1. i	1. joust
2. j	2. irascible
3. f	3. lament
4. a	4. intervene
5. h	5. laconic
6. e	6. insouciant
7. c	7. inveigled
8. g	8. languish
9. d	9. lassitude
10. b	10. karma

REVIEW #20, page 234

Matching:	Fill in the Blank:
1. c	1. marauders
2. d	2. loiter
3. a	3. lexicon
4. b	4. legacy
5. i	5. maimed
6. g	6. lax
7. e	7. laudable
8. j	8. lieu
9. h	9. lesions
10. f	10. Lethargy

REVIEW #21, page 245

Matching:	Fill in the Blank:
1. c	1. mirages
2. a	2. Marshaling
3. b	3. milieu
4. i	4. menagerie
5. j	5. misnomer
6. f	6. masticate
7. h	7. migratory
8. d	8. martyr
9. g	9. misanthropy
10. e	10. melancholy

REVIEW #22, page 256

Matching:	Fill in the Blank:
1. d	1. mustered
2. c	2. oblique
3. e	3. nepotism
4. a	4. muse
5. g	5. myriad
6. f	6. obtuse
7. j	7. mode
8. b	8. noxious
9. h	9. mores
10. i	10. noisome

REVIEW #23, page 267

Matching:	Fill in the Blank:
1. h	1. ostracized
2. c	2. parried
3. b	3. partitioned
4. a	4. ousted
5. g	5. penitent
6. d	6. optimum
7. f	7. orthodox
8. e	8. paranoia
9. j	9. opportune
10. i	10. paradox

REVIEW #24, page 278

Matching:	Fill in the Blank:
1. b	1. photogenic
2. c	2. periphery
3. e	3. petulant
4. i	4. perverse
5. d	5. philanthropy
6. h	6. permeated
7. g	7. piqued
8. j	8. pied
9. a	9. pillaged
10. f	10. phobia

REVIEW #25, page 289

Matching:
1. d
2. g
3. a
4. c
5. b
6. j
7. i
8. e
9. h
10. f

Fill in the Blank:
1. prowess
2. procrastinated
3. queues
4. precarious
5. quandary
6. potentate
7. propulsive
8. porcine
9. proficient
10. plight

REVIEW #26, page 300

Matching:
1. h
2. j
3. a
4. i
5. e
6. b
7. d
8. g
9. f
10. c

Fill in the Blank:
1. remorse
2. ramification
3. roster
4. quirk
5. quixotic
6. riveted
7. relinquish
8. resurgent
9. reminisce
10. revered

REVIEW #27, page 311

Matching:
1. g
2. j
3. h
4. c
5. e
6. b
7. i
8. a
9. f
10. d

Fill in the Blank:
1. serpentine
2. segregate
3. somber
4. scrutinized
5. scapegoat
6. sonorous
7. stupefied
8. spurned
9. rudimentary
10. spurred

REVIEW #28, page 322

Matching:	Fill in the Blank:
1. d	1. tethered
2. j	2. torque
3. a	3. truncated
4. e	4. surfeit
5. f	5. sundry
6. h	6. supplanted
7. i	7. trenchant
8. g	8. truculent
9. c	9. ubiquitous
10. b	10. tyro

REVIEW #29, page 333

Matching:	Fill in the Blank:
1. d	1. verbatim
2. f	2. withered
3. g	3. wrest
4. c	4. unbridled
5. j	5. vertigo
6. h	6. veered
7. i	7. yore
8. a	8. umbrage
9. b	9. volition
10. e	10. waning

Word List

abhor, 15
abominate, 16
abridge, 17
abstruse, 18
abut, 19
abyss, 20
accolade, 21
adjunct, 22
affidavit, 23
affinity, 24
Review #1, 25

aftermath, 26
aggrandize, 27
ajar, 28
alienate, 29
alleviate, 30
allure, 31
aloof, 32
also-ran, 33
altercation, 34
alternative, 35
Review #2, 36

ambiance, 37
amenable, 38
amplify, 39
antecedent, 40
anterior, 41
appalling, 42
aptitude, 43
archaic, 44
arduous, 45
artisan, 46
Review #3, 47

askew, 48
aspire, 49
assuage, 50
astute, 51
asunder, 52
atrophy, 53
atypical, 54
austere, 55
badger, 56
ballistics, 57
Review #4, 58

balm, 59
beget, 60
beleaguer, 61
bereave, 62
beset, 63
bizarre, 64
blather, 65
bleak, 66
bludgeon, 67
bucolic, 68
Review #5, 69

bulwark, 70
cache, 71
cacophony, 72
cajole, 73
callous, 74
callow, 75
candor, 76
capacious, 77
castigate, 78
catapult, 79
Review #6, 80

catharsis, 81
caucus, 82
cerebral, 83
certify, 84
chasm, 85
chattel, 86
chide, 87
chronic, 88
circa, 89
citadel, 90
Review #7, 91

claimant, 92
cloister, 93
commodious, 94
comprise 95
congenial, 96
connoisseur, 97
consensus, 98
coterie, 99
countenance, 100
coup 101
Review #8, 102

couture, 103
cower, 104
cranny, 105
craven, 106
creditor, 107
criterion, 108
cubism, 109
curtail, 110
curvilinear, 111
damper, 112
Review #9, 113

BOCA RATON PUBLIC LIBRARY, FLORIDA

3 3656 0423939 0

Other Books Available from New Monic Books:

Vocabulary Cartoons, Elementary Edition
ISBN# 0965242277 - $12.95

Vocabulary Cartoons II, SAT Word Power
ISBN# 0965242242 - $12.95

The Unofficial SAT Word Dictionary
ISBN# 0965242250 - $12.95

Attention Teachers

Blackline masters and overhead transparencies are available for all Vocabulary Cartoon books.

Quantity discounts for all books are also available.

For more information:
Call **1 800 741-1295** or look us up on the web at
www.vocabularycartoons.com

New Monic Books, Inc.
P.O. Box 511314
Punta Gorda, FL 33951

J 428.2 Voc
Vocabulary cartoons :